I HEARD LIFE CALLING ME

I HEARD LIFE CALLING ME
Poems of Yi Sŏng-bok

TRANSLATORS

HYE-JIN JUHN
GEORGE SIDNEY

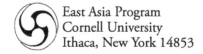

East Asia Program
Cornell University
Ithaca, New York 14853

The Cornell East Asia Series is published by the Cornell University East Asia Program (distinct from Cornell University Press). We publish books on a variety of scholarly topics relating to East Asia as a service to the academic community and the general public. Standing Orders, which provide for automatic notification and invoicing of each title in the series upon publication are accepted.

If after review by internal and external readers a manuscript is accepted for publication, it is published on the basis of camera-ready copy provided by the author who is responsible for any copyediting and manuscript formatting. Alternative arrangements should be made with approval of the Series. Address submission inquiries to CEAS Editorial Board, East Asia Program, Cornell University, Ithaca, New York 14853-7601.

The translation and publication of this volume was supported by the Korean Literature Translation Institute.

Number 145 in the Cornell East Asia Series
Copyright ©2010 by George Sidney and Hye-jin Juhn Sidney. All rights reserved.
ISSN: 1050-2955
ISBN: 978-1-933947-15-0 hc
ISBN: 978-1-933947-45-7 pb
Library of Congress Control Number: 2009925878
Printed in the United States of America
24 23 22 21 20 19 18 17 16 15 14 13 12 11   9 8 7 6 5 4 3 2

The paper in this book meets the requirements for permanence of ISO 9706:1994.

Contents

Index of Poems

남해 금산 / South Sea, Silk Mountain

I Heard Life Calling Me

Translators' Preface

The poems selected here include all those mentioned by Professors Hwang Tong-kyu and Kim Hyŏn in their commentaries (see Appendixes 2 and 3 in this volume) that appeared in the first editions of *When Does a Rolling Stone Awaken* and *South Sea, Silk Mountain.* The order of the poems is that presented in the first editions.

Korean orthography does not distinguish between upper and lower-case letters. We have used lower-case throughout, except for the pronoun "I," proper names, and family members when addressed in dialogue (Mom, Dad). We've preserved as much as possible, given the differences in sentence structure and word order of Korean and English, the physical shape of the poems on the page.

In the few instances that we have chosen, for semantic and/or aesthetic reasons, to romanize rather than translate a Korean word, we've explained the meaning of the word in the Notes. An example: the common English translation of the Korean vegetable *mu* is "radish," a word that connotes to a Western reader the small, red, globular, somewhat piquant vegetable used primarily in salads, whereas *mu* is white, long, thick and tapered like a giant carrot, a valuable cash crop and a basic ingredient of Korean food and diet.

We have strived to preserve the poetic quality of the original, to have the poems read in English as the fine poetry they are in Korean. When uncertain about the nuances of words or phrases, we consulted the author.

Our thanks to the Korean Literature Translation Institute for its grant award; to Mai Shaikhanuar-Cota, Managing Editor of the Cornell East Asia Series, for her unflagging support, patience, and editorial counsel; and to Yi Sŏng-bok, for his exquisite poetry, his trust, his friendship.

We would also like to express our thanks to the editors of the following publications, in which several of our translations of Yi Sŏng-bok's poems first appeared: *The Marlboro Review*, the *International Poetry Review*, *The Literary Review*, and the *Sycamore Review*.

Introduction

Yi Sŏng-bok has been hailed as one of the most important contemporary South Korean poets. He has been credited by scholars and critics with having innovated a new poetic style that opened a fresh path for modernist poetry in Korea, and that strongly influenced and inspired younger poets. He has published five collections of poetry and received three of the country's most prestigious literary awards. "There haven't been many cases in Korea," the critic Chŏng Hyo-ku wrote of him, "in which a poet attracted so much attention from so many people, and was so quickly and willingly accepted as the representative voice of the time. . . . Like a doctor, he diagnosed the traumas afflicting the society, and so made his readers—the patients, his fellow contemporaries . . . the young educated people of the time—aware of their own traumas. They were shocked by what they discovered."[1]

Yi was born in 1952, during the Korean War, in Sangju, a small country town in central Korea some hundred miles south of Seoul. He was the second son, the fourth of five children in a staunchly Protestant family. A bright, motivated student, with a talent for writing and a penchant for being different, he early developed an interest in European literature. He studied German in high school, majored in French at Seoul National University where, after fulfilling his obligatory military service in the Republic of Korea Navy, he went on to earn a bachelor's, master's, and doctoral degrees in French Language and Literature. He wrote his master's thesis on Charles Baudelaire and his doctoral dissertation on Gérard de Nerval.

Yi was one of a group of talented young poets who came of age during the 1970s,[2] a turbulent decade in which South Korea was undergoing a rapid, forced transition from the third-world agrarian nation it then was toward the urban, technologically sophisticated post-industrial society it has become. The populace was subjected to intense stress, to wrenching transitions and dislocations. There was mass displacement of individuals and families from farm to factory, from rural to urban life; there was the growth of a small, powerful nouveau-riche capitalist class; there was the highly visible and corrupting presence of some forty thousand American soldiers stationed at military bases in Seoul and throughout the country—all compounded by oppressively authoritarian governments, civilian and military, and an ever-present fear and tension produced by the iciest of cold-war confrontations with North Korea.

Yi's poetry began appearing in Korean literary magazines in the late 1970s, beginning with the publication by the journal *Literature and Intelligence Quarterly* (문학과 지성사) in 1977 of his poem "in a congenial brothel."

When Does a Rolling Stone Awaken

Yi's first collection of poems, *When Does a Rolling Stone Awaken* (딩구는 돌은 언제 잠깨는가), published in 1980, is a trenchant critique of the state of mind of Koreans and of the social and political conditions in the country at the time. It was an immediate success. Critics and the general public responded enthusiastically. Yi was praised for his intellectual humor, his iconoclasm, his cynical view of society and contemporary civilization.

The poems, the distinguished poet and Seoul National University professor Hwang Tong-kyu wrote, were unlike any that Korean readers had become accustomed to.[3] Yi had experimented with form and syntax, fractured cohesiveness, fragmented lines and phrases, dispensed with punctuation, violated traditional grammatical rules and linguistic patterns. He incorporated dialogue and broken snatches of conversation, montaged and juxtaposed unrelated, often disturbingly grotesque images. He made use of abrupt disconnections and shifts of focus, of the fluidity of free association and the stream of consciousness, of dreams and dream sequences, of surrealistic configurations of reality, of black humor. The effect was an estranging defamiliarization of the familiar that drew attention to and illuminated for people the reality of their lives and of the world in which they were living.

Commenting on the difference, Yi explained that

> unlike most Korean poets, who began writing with echoes in mind of Kim So-wŏl and Han Yong-un, the only Korean poet influential for me at that time was Kim Su-yŏng. More influential for me at that early stage were Celan, Mandelstam, Pavese, Dylan Thomas, the French symbolist poets, especially Baudelaire. I borrowed a lot from other foreign writers: Kafka, Dostoevsky, Thomas Mann, Proust, Nietzsche. For example, in regard to social and political situations, I adopted Kafka's model—the relationship between father and son, the idea of seeing the family structure as a microcosm of society, the idea of seeking realism through symbols. These ideas weren't too familiar to many Koreans at the time. I also introduced the technique of combining words and ideas in such a way that they would have powerfully destructive effects. My use of that technique to portray Korean situations, and my developing the idea that the ordinary life of an individual could be conceived as a reflection of the social and political situation was also new.

What I was doing was probably what Korean critics now call deconstruction, a word that didn't exist at that time. But compared to the deconstruction they discuss these days, which is more philosophical and ideological, my deconstruction was more practical and realistic.[4]

Although he used Western surrealistic literary devices to communicate his vision of the unreality of the times, the poems are rooted in the tangible realities of Korean life. His images are consistently colloquial and concrete: "a mother like a bale of rice straw, a sister with a smile like popped kernels of rice" ("Moraenae • 1978," p. 79); regrets "as thick as a swarm of customers at a grubby bar," mouths "like the windows of junked cars" ("again, in a congenial brothel," p. 143); a road "flat like dried squid" ("exodus," p. 35); "memories like blood pudding dumplings" ("excursion," p. 41); a plane ripping the sky "like a surgical saw" ("the summer mountain," p. 51); a body "not worth more than a pair of shoes" ("a journal of love," p. 111); people getting along "the way hairs nest among hairs" ("to my son," p. 121); "shame, like rusty nails . . . hammered into the walls" ("execution," p. 135); paradise the "window of a brothel" ("a journal of ignorance," p. 107).

Self-reflective and highly personal, the poems span a period of some twenty years, from recollections of childhood sensations and experiences dating roughly from 1959, when Yi was seven years old, to shortly before the government's violent repression in 1980 of democratic protest in the city of Kwangju.

The narrator of the poems is in his mid-to-late twenties, as was Yi when he wrote them. He is educated, sensitive, apathetic, cynical, wryly sardonic. His tone of voice ranges from matter-of-fact ironic understatement to caustic sarcasm to pained outrage. At times he appears to be speaking to the public, at times either to himself or to an "other" (seemingly a woman). He perceives himself inhabiting a world turned upside-down, an unreal world in which the "normal," rational order has come undone. Nature behaves unnaturally. Trees produce fruit before they bloom, fish fly, dead fish rain down from the sky, flower petals turn to claws. Things happen randomly, unpredictably, without logical cause-effect linkages. The country is sick. The environment is polluted. Corruption—public and personal—is widespread. Families are breaking apart, violence, poverty, depravity abound. That people are oblivious of or indifferent to the sickness permeating the culture, that they have so accommodated themselves to conditions in the country as to accept them as normal, is a major theme of the book. Secure in their "congenial brothel"—a metaphor that frames the book—like rolling stones they tumble aimlessly along, insensate. "All were sick . . ." the narrator in the poem "that day" says, "but nobody felt the pain" (p. 87).

For the narrator, pain—physical, moral, psychological, existential—is palpable, a chronic condition of life at the time. "If you consume all your loneliness today," the poem "exodus" (p. 35) begins, "you won't have any pain left to chew on tomorrow"; in the poem "excursion" (p. 39), the narrator makes a trip to a city named "Pain"; in the "the river never returns" (p. 49), "pain [is] sold in the street."

Pain is especially acute in the poems about family—poignantly sad childhood reminiscences of loss and familial disintegration—and in the bittersweet (more bitter than sweet) poems about love.[5] The societal sickness has eaten away at the bonds of all human relationships, creating distance between people, afflicting parents and children, afflicting lovers, making love so very difficult to come by. In the book's last poem, when love does come, it comes "at the wrong time, too late."

From the "spring [that] did not come" of the first poem to "the love that came . . . too late" of the last poem, a sense of loss, and of longing for what has been lost—innocence, home, self, friends, family, love, human decency, the past—pervades the book. The narrator dreams, fantasizes, that there is a better, a sane, rational, uncorrupted world outside the congenial brothel, "a country far away" (oral tale, p. 31), "the country without violence . . . where people . . . get along the way hairs nest among hairs" ("to my son," p. 121), "the country where neither the body nor the heart aches" ("again, in a congenial brothel," p. 147). He knows there is no such place, that paradise, once lost, is lost forever.

South Sea, Silk Mountain

Yi's second collection of poems, *South Sea, Silk Mountain* (남해 금산), published six years later, is a softer, quieter, more intimate book. The poems are shorter. With few exceptions they are in a lyrical rather than a narrative mode. The tone is less caustic, the images less surrealistically grotesque, the content more philosophical and spiritual. The rural settings—fields, rice paddies, woods and forests, rivers and streams—are more natural, more romantic than the cityscapes of *When Does a Rolling Stone Awaken.*

"One reason for the shift of tone and focus," Yi said, "is that when I was writing the poems in the first book, society was in political chaos. It was dominated by irrationalities. People were being victimized and arrested. When I was writing the poems in the second book, the social situation had improved. Another reason is that as I got older, I became more interested in human existence than in social issues. . . . The world of the first book is a predominantly male world, the world of the father, my own father, the father of all people, God, a world where bad myths and symbols are rampant; the world of the second book is the world of the mother, who changes all the garbage in the world into clear fountain water."[6]

In contrast to the traditional portrayal of the mother in the first book as weak, passively suffering, to be pitied, in *South Sea, Silk Mountain* she is strong, nurturing, protective, both Earth Mother and Holy Mother. She comforts her shamed and humiliated daughter, she alleviates the anguish of her narrator son, extracts the nails "lodged deep within [his] hands and feet and

I Heard Life Calling Me

chest" ("mother 1," p. 203). Yi said that when writing the poems he was obsessed by motherness, that though one cannot obliterate shame, one can get consolation from the mother. "Mother is where all begins, is the only hope."[7]

Shame and humiliation are dominant themes in the book. The narrator is afflicted by a sense of shame so profound that he feels it etched upon his back like a tortoiseshell ("shame, like a tortoiseshell," p. 171), feels it as a long glittering chain dragging along behind him ("what was far away falls like raindrops," p. 175). The shame is personal, for "the wrongdoing I did in my time, that can't be forgiven [that] hurts like a nail in my forehead" ("white flower lanterns on tall trees," p. 235); it is familial, especially for his humiliated sister, a victim of rape and possibly incest; and it is national, for his country, for things that happened "too shameful to talk about . . . shameful even for those who did not take part" ("and again the fog descended," p. 169).

As in *When Does a Rolling Stone Awaken*, the narrator— here referred to by Yi as "a poetic narrator, in the manner of Baudelaire, Nerval, and Proust,"—is again on the road, on a "journey of anguished wandering," a quest for the love of the woman he loves, for the lost paradise of the first book.[8]

The journey is also a rite of passage for the narrator, a spiritual descent within, into the "catacomb of memory" where "there is no peace" ("no peace in memory," p. 163). In the course of the journey he attains a measure of enlightenment, becoming increasingly aware of the impossibility of recovering what has been lost, of his mortality, of the imminence and the inevitability of death.

Both journey and book end at the Silk Mountain (*kŭmsan*) by the South Sea (*namhae*), where the narrator comes upon the woman he has been seeking. She has been immured in stone. "For her love," he says,

I followed her into the stone
one summer it rained a lot

weeping, she left the stone
led by sun and moon she left
I'm alone now at the edge of the blue sky
    above Silk Mountain by the South Sea
alone I sink into the blue water of the South Sea
    at Silk Mountain. [9]

Other Works

Yi's third and fourth collections of poetry, *That Summer's End* (그 여름의 끝, 1990) and *Memories of the Holly Tree* (호랑가시 나무의 기억, 1993), continue the inward movement of *South Sea, Silk Mountain*: away from external violence and toward normal, everyday domesticity. Family is the basic frame in both books, in which Yi expresses his "yearning for the maternal and the feminine . . . a yearning, a seeking for what is precious and dear in life . . . that which remains beneath the ashes after a house has burned to the ground."[10]

The poems of *That Summer's End*—"love letters," he called them—are about the relationship between "self" (the narrator) and "other" (the lover). The poems of *Memories of the Holly Tree* are about family relations, about children and spouses, "about how I," Yi said, "a married man now, understand the world as father and husband. So it contains a series of ordinary events that occur to ordinary people in their ordinary lives. The third book is essentially contemplative in a Confucian manner . . . and has at its core the healing of life by means of Eastern philosophical thought. The fourth book, which contains many Buddhist elements, shows the change I'd undergone after my second stay in Paris."[11]

Ah, Mouthless Things (아, 입이 없는 것들), Yi's fifth collection, published in 2004, ten years after *Memories of the Holly Tree*, is about "the fundamental issues . . . the structure of life, in which humans, like all living creatures, are interconnected, to eat and be eaten."[12] His darkest and most philosophical book, it reflects his growing interest in psychoanalysis and cognitive psychology as well as his existential despair at what he perceives to be the human condition. He postulates a naturalistic world, "ruled by four elements: sex, eating, birth, death," by which all life is bound, to which all life is subject.[13] The narrator, tormented by his inability to master the animalism of his hunger and sexuality, which he feels has poisoned him, body and soul, struggles, unsuccessfully, to free himself from the demonic violence he feels both within and in the world around him, to escape himself and that world he didn't choose and, like the narrator of *When Does a Rolling Stone Awaken*, to find peace.[14]

In 1982, Yi was honored with the Kim Su-yŏng Literary Award for *When Does a Rolling Stone Awaken*; in 1990, with the Sowŏl Poetry Award for *That Summer's End*; in 2004, with the Daesan Literary Award for *Ah, Mouthless Things*.

His poems have appeared in American and French literary journals and reviews. A French translation of *South Sea, Silk Mountain* was published in 2004.[15]

In 2005, the quarterly journal *The Poet's World* (시인세계) asked one hundred fifty-six South Korean poets to list their favorite books of Korean poetry. *When Does a Rolling Stone Awaken* placed fourth overall, first among the work of poets still living.[16]

Since 1981, Yi has been a member of the faculty at Keimyung University in Taegu, where he teaches Creative Writing and French literature.

Notes

1. Chŏng Hyo-ku, 정효구, "신화의 안과 바깥—이성복 론," *상상력의 모험—1980 년대의 시인들*, p. 169. Here is a representative sampling of the many articles and essays that have been and continue to be written about Yi and his work:

Chang Sŏk-ju, "방법론적 부드러움의 시학—이성복을 중심으로 한 80년대 시의 한 흐름," *한 완벽주의자의 책 읽기*, 청하, 1987, pp. 54–55.

Kim Hyŏn, "따뜻한 비관주의—이성복의 시세계," *젊은 시인들의 상상세계/말들의 풍경*, 문학과 지성사, 1985, pp. 138–140.

Kim Yong- rak, "문학에 천재는 없다," *현대시*, 1호, 1999.

Pak Hyŏng-jun, "뱀의 입속에 모가지만 남은 개구리가 허공에 하는 고백," *작가세계*, 58호, 가을, 2003.

Yi Kyŏng-ho, "이성복 편," *대표시평론 II*, 실천문학, 2000, pp. 121–122.

Yi Nam-ho, "1980년대 시의 발달," *문학의 시대*, 1호, 풀빛, 1983.

Yi Sŏng-ha, "정보화 시대를 사는 시인들의 정신과 위상," *한국 현대 대표시선*, 이진 출판사, 2000, pp. 267–272.

Yi Sŭng-hun, "1970년대 한국 모더니즘 시의 전개," *한국 모더니즘 시사*, 문예사, 2000, pp. 291–297.

Chŏng Hyo-ku, "신화의 안과 바깥—이성복 론," *상상력의 모험—1980 년대의 시인들*, 민음사, 1992, pp. 167–178.

2. Yi Nam-ho, U Ch'ang-je, Yi Kwang-ho, and Kim Mi-hyun, *Twentieth Century Korean Literature,* trans. Ryu Young-ju, edited by Brother Anthony of T'aizé (Norwalk: Eastbridge Signature Books, 2002), pp. 72–75. The group of poets include Hwang Chi-u, Ch'oe Sŭng-ho, Pak Nam-ch'ŏl, Ch'oe Sŭng-ja, Kim Hye-sun, and Chang Chŏng-il.

3. Hwang Tong-kyu, Appendix 2, p. 250.

4. Translators' interview, conducted in Taegu, October 13, 2003. Appendix 1 contains excerpts of the interview.

5. Poems about family: a road to Kŭmch'on; flowering dad; a family scene; an account of a fight; Moraenae, 1978. Poems about love: Christmas; a journal of

love; about time; again, in a congenial brothel; now only about love that came at the wrong time, too late.

6. Translators' interview. Another contributing factor might well be his turning away from Western influences. In 1984 Yi went to France. He stayed a year, mostly in Aix-en-Provence. During his year there his enthusiasm for Western literature diminished. He turned away from the West and toward the East. "I rejected Baudelaire and Nietzsche. When I went to live in France in 1984, I looked forward to experiencing what I'd read in the books, but I was extremely disappointed. I longed to confirm my identity and so I studied Asian philosophy. The essence of that philosophy is yin and yang: love, love of things, of nature, of people."

7. French translators' interview: No Mi-sug and Alain Génetoit, "Entretien avec Lee Seong-bok [sic]," *Poesie*, № 111, Éditions Belin (Paris), 2005, p. 70.

8. Ibid, pp. 68–69. Yi said that the poetic narrator is perhaps the incarnation of Christ, that there is always in his poetry a quest for the Holy Grail, and that though the central focus in each of his five books is different, "in each there is a journey, and the five together constitute a journey that continues to evolve: father, mother, love, family, the world. In all five the journey is the same—a quest for the meaning of life."

9. The South Sea is the Korean Strait, the body of water at the southern tip of the peninsula. It connects the East Sea (Sea of Japan) and the West Sea (East China Sea). Silk Mountain is the 2,300-foot high Mount Kŭm, on the island of Namhae, in the South Sea. The famous Buddhist monk Won-hyo built a temple there in 686 CE. Legend has it that Yi Sŏng-gye, the founder and first king (Sejo) of the Chosŏn dynasty (1392–1910) changed its name to Mount Kŭm. Legend has it that he prayed at the temple for 100 days, promising that if he was successful in overthrowing the kingdom of Koryo, he would cover the mountain in silk.

10. Translators' interview.

11. Ibid. Yi went to Paris in 1991 on a Yonam Foundation grant.

12. Translators' interview

13. French translators' interview, p. 70.

14. "Cynicism and pessimism," Yi has said, "have always been the motifs of my imagination. I have always seen the world pessimistically. But my pessimism isn't nihilistic, it's different from nihilism. You struggle, knowing you are going to lose, that you are doomed to fail. That is an affirmation of human dignity. Struggling while knowing I'm going to lose is the main theme of my life and my poetry."

15. *Des choses qui viennent après la douleur*, No Mi-Sug and Alain Génetiot, trans., Éditions Belin (Paris, France), 2005.

16. *When Does a Rolling Stone Awaken* was chosen after Paek Sŏk's *Deer* (사슴), Kim Su-yŏng's *Enormous Roots* (거대한 뿌리), Chŏng Chi-yong's *Poems of Chŏng Chi-yong* (정지용 시집), and before Sŏ Chŏng-ju's *Flower Snake* (꽃뱀). To have been ranked with four poets of their stature is further affirmation of Yi's continuing influence on contemporary South Korean poetry.

I Heard Life Calling Me

POEMS FROM

When Does a Rolling Stone Awaken

1959 년

그해 겨울이 지나고 여름이 시작되어도
봄은 오지 않았다 복숭아나무는
채 꽃 피기 전에 아주 작은 열매를 맺고
不姙의 살구나무는 시들어 갔다
소년들의 性器에는 까닭없이 고름이 흐르고
의사들은 아프리카까지 移民을 떠났다 우리는
유학 가는 친구들에게 술 한잔 얻어 먹거나
이차 대전 때 南洋으로 징용 간 삼촌에게서
뜻밖의 편지를 받기도 했다 그러나 어떤
놀라움도 우리를 無氣力과 不感症으로부터
불러내지 못했고 다만, 그 전해에 비해
약간 더 화려하게 절망적인 우리의 습관을
修飾했을 뿐 아무 것도 追憶되지 않았다
어머니는 살아 있고 여동생은 발랄하지만
그들의 기쁨은 소리 없이 내 구둣발에 짓이겨
지거나 이미 파리채 밑에 으깨어져 있었고
春畵를 볼 때마다 부패한 채 떠올라 왔다
그해 겨울이 지나고 여름이 시작되어도
우리는 봄이 아닌 倫理와 사이비 學說과
싸우고 있었다 오지 않는 봄이어야 했기에
우리는 보이지 않는 監獄으로 자진해 갔다

1959

that year, though winter ended and summer began
spring did not come   the peach tree
bore tiny fruits before flowering
and the barren apricot withered
for unknown reasons pus oozed from the penises of young boys
and doctors emigrated as far as Africa   we were treated to drinks by
friends leaving to study abroad
and out of the blue a letter arrived from an uncle drafted
and sent to the South Pacific during World War Two   but there were
no surprises to roust us from our indifference and apathy
and other than glamorizing,
even more than last year, our habitual depression,
we did nothing worth remembering
mom was still alive and my younger sister full of life,
yet without a peep from them their happiness was squashed,
beneath my shoes, by flyswatters—a memory that surfaced,
rotten, whenever I saw a salacious picture
though winter ended and summer began
it wasn't the spring we wrestled with, but ethics
and false theories   it was a spring that did not come,
and so we voluntarily went off to an invisible jail

정든 유곽에서

1

누이가 듣는 音樂 속으로 늦게 들어오는
男子가 보였다 나는 그게 싫었다 내 音樂은
죽음 이상으로 침침해서 발이 빠져 나가지
못하도록 雜草 돋아나는데, 그 남자는
누구일까 누이의 戀愛는 아름다와도 될까
의심하는 가운데 잠이 들었다

牧丹이 시드는 가운데 地下의 잠, 韓半島가
　소심한 물살에 시달리다가 흘러들었다 伐木
당한 女子의 반복되는 臨終, 병을 돌보던
　靑春이 그때마다 나를 흔들어 깨워도 가난한
몸은 고결하였고 그래서 죽은 체했다
잠자는 동안 내 祖國의 신체를 지키는 자는 누구인가
日本인가, 日蝕인가 나의 헤픈 입에서
욕이 나왔다 누이의 戀愛는 아름다와도 될까
파리가 잉잉거리는 하숙집의 아침에

2

엘리, 엘리 죽지 말고 내 목마른 裸身에 못박혀요
얼마든지 죽을 수 있어요 몸은 하나지만
참한 죽음 하나 당신이 가꾸어 꽃을
보여 주세요 엘리, 엘리 당신이 昇天하면
나는 죽음으로 越境할 뿐 더럽힌 몸으로 죽어서도
시집 가는 당신의 딸, 당신의 어머니

in a congenial brothel

1

one night, late, I saw a man enter the music
my sister was listening to   I didn't like that   my music
is as grave as death   weeds sprout from it, tangling
my feet   and who is
that man   can this love of my sister's be beautiful
wondering, I fell asleep

while I slept underground, peonies withered   the Korean peninsula,
tossed about on choppy waters, sailed on   a woman, cut down like a
tree, died over and over again   and at each dying my youthful self,
tending her hurts, tried to waken me, but though destitute I was
patrician by birth, and so pretended to be dead   while I sleep, who
tends the body of my country
those from the land where the sun rises?   those who eclipsed that sun?
profanity spewed from my profligate mouth
can this love of my sister's be beautiful
morning, a house of rented bedrooms, flies nosing about

2

Eli, Eli please do not die   be nailed to my naked parched body
though you have only one body, you're able to die as often as you
choose   a death of substance   please show me the flowers you raised
Eli, Eli when you ascend to heaven I'll cross over into death, and that's
it   the spoiled body of your daughter—your mother—will be married
off, even after she dies

(continued)

정든 유곽에서

3
그리고 나의 별이 무겁게 숨 쉬는 소리를
들을 수 있다 혈관 마디마다 더욱
붉어지는 呻吟, 어두운 살의 하늘을
날으는 방패연, 눈을 감고 쳐다보는
까마득한 별

그리고 나의 별이 파닥거리는 까닭을
말할 수 있다 봄밤의 노곤한 무르팍에
머리를 눕히고 달콤한 노래 부를 때,
戰爭과 굶주림이 아주 멀리 있을 때
유순한 革命처럼 깃발 날리며
새벽까지 行進하는 나의 별

그리고 별은 나의 祖國에서만 별이라
불릴 것이다 별이라 불리기에 後世
찬란할 것이다 백설탕과 식빵처럼
口味를 바꾸고도 광대뼈에 반짝이는
나의 별, 우리 韓族의 별

in a congenial brothel

3
and I can hear the labored breathing
of my star   its groans grow redder
at every juncture of my veins   a shield-shaped kite flies
in a flesh-dark sky   eyes closed, I can see
my distant star

and I can tell you why it glitters
as I sing a sweet song,
my head in the lap of the languid spring night,
war and hunger far far away
my star sails on till dawn
a flag aloft, the banner of a peaceful revolution

and in no other country is the word for star *pyŏl*
and for that reason our *pyŏl* will glow on for our future generations
and even after we've succumbed
to white bread and sugar, on our cheekbones
my star will still be shining—the *pyŏl* of our Korean people

봄 밤

잎이 나기 전에 꽃을 내뱉는 살구나무,
중얼거리며 좁은 뜰을 빠져 나가고
노곤한 담벼락을 슬픔이 윽박지르면
꿈도, 방향도 없이 서까래가 넘어지고
보이지 않는 칼에 네 종아리가 잘려 나가고
가까이 입을 다문 채 컹컹 짖는 中年 남자들
네 발목, 손목에 가래가 고인다, 벌써 어두워!

봄밤엔 어릴 때 던져 올린 사금파리가
네 얼굴에 박힌다
봄밤엔 별을 보지 않아도 돼,
네 얼굴이 더욱 빛나 아프잖아?
봄밤엔 잠자면서 오줌을 누어야 해
겨우내 밀린 오줌을, 꼭, 그러나
이마는 물처럼 흐르고
미끄러운 유리 입술,

벽은 뚫고 나가기엔 너무 두껍고
누군가 새어들 만큼 얇아
아무래도 네 영혼은 누, 눈 감고 아, 아, 아웅하기

spring night

the apricot tree spits out blossoms before leaves,
and with a mumble crosses the narrow garden
when sadness shouts at the weary wall
the roof beam, without direction or a dream, falls
and the calf of your leg is sliced by an unseen sword
nearby middle-aged men woof doglike through closed mouths
phlegm collects on your ankles and wrists   already it's dark!

on a spring night the shard of broken pottery you hurled at the sky
when a child
returns and embeds itself in your face
on a spring night there's no need to look at the stars
your face shines so much brighter   it hurts, doesn't it?
on a spring night you ought to pee in your sleep,
the pee you've been saving up all winter, for sure
but your forehead's smooth as flowing water
and your lips are slick as glass,

the wall's too thick for you to breach, yet thin enough
for someone to slip through to you   anyway, it's your soul that closes
its eyes and p . . . p . . . plays guess who

또 비가 오고

또 비가 오고 잠 없는 肉身은 집을 나선다
또 비가 오고 죽은 물고기는 하늘에서 떨어진다
또 실성한 봄은 여물지 않은 복숭아 속에서 중얼거리고
날벌레들이 서로 몸을 더듬는다
또 우는 아이의 턱이 목에서 빠져 나가고
슬픔이 괴로움을 만나 흐린 물이 된다

부패와 분노가 만나 불이 되고
사내와 계집이 만나 땀이 되어도
못 만난 것들은 뿔뿔이 江을 따라 간다
한 번 죽은 누이는 거듭 죽는다

빨리 오너라 비 오는 밤 通禁을 깨고
빨리 오너라 後金의 아내여 와서
톱밥과 발톱을 섞어 떡을 만들라
앉은뱅이와 곱추를 불러 동요를 부르게 하라
늙은 王과 송충이를 교미시켜 病든 아들을 얻게 하라
빨리 오너라 비 오는 밤 횃대에 올라 순한 닭들과 더불어
　　노래하라

again it rains

again it rains and a sleepless body leaves home
again it rains and a dead fish falls from the sky
again the deranged spring mumbles inside an unripe peach
and gnats grope each other's bodies
again the chin drops from the neck of a crying child
and sadness and pain conjoin and become muddy water

corruption and anger conjoin and become fire
males and females conjoin and become sweat
but things that don't conjoin go separately, following the river
a dead sister dies again

come quickly, on this rainy night break the curfew
come quickly, wife of Hugŭm   come
and mix sawdust and toenails and make *ttŏk*
call for a cripple and a hunchback and have them sing children's songs
mate an old king and a caterpillar and have them beget a sickly son
come quickly   on this rainy night roost with the placid chickens
    and sing along with them

루우트 기호 속에서

바퀴벌레들이 동요하고 있어 꿈이 떠내려가고 있어
가라앉는 山, 길이 벌떡 일어섰어 구름은 땅 밑에서
빨리 흐르고 어릴 때 돌로 쳐죽인 뱀이 나를
감고 있어 개벌레가 뜯어 먹는 뺨, 썩은 나무를
감는 덩굴손, 죽음은 꼬리를 흔들며 반기고 있어
<<딸아, 이틀만 나를 다시 품에 안아 줘
<<아들아, 이틀만 나를 데리고 놀아 줘
<<가슴아, 이틀만 뛰지 말아 줘
밥상 위, 튀긴 물고기가 퍼덕인다 밥상 위, 미나리와
쑥갓이 꽃핀다 전에 훔쳐 먹은 노란 사과 하나
몸 속을 굴러다닌다 불을 끄고 숨을 멈춰도 달아날 데가
　없어
<<엄마, 배불리 먹고 나니 눈물이 눈을 몰아내네
<<엄마, 내 가려운 몸을 구워 줘, 두려워
<<엄마, 落伍된 엄마, 내 발자국을 지워 줘
얼마나 걸었을까 엄마의 입술이 은행나무 가지에
걸려 있었어 겁 많은 江이 거슬러 올라가다
불길이 되었어 時計가 깨어지고 말갈족과 흉노족들이
횃불로 몸 지지며 춤추고 있었어 性器 끝에서
번개가 빠져나가고 떨어진 어둠은 엄청나게 무거웠어

inside the square root sign

cockroaches are stirring   a dream is floating away   a mountain sinks
a road leaps straight up   clouds move fast beneath the ground   the
snake I killed when I was young is coiling around me   cheeks being
gnawed by sesame bugs, tendrils coiling around a rotting tree, death
wagging its tail, welcoming   "chicken, please sit on me again for a
   couple of days"
"son, please play with me for a couple of days"
"my heart, please don't beat for a couple of days"
on the dining table a fried fish flips and flops   on the dining table,
dandelions and a daisy bloom   the one yellow apple I stole and ate
long ago rolls around inside my body   even if I turn off the light and
stop breathing there's no place to escape to
"Mom, now that I've eaten well my tears are pushing out my eyeballs"
"Mom, please roast my itching body   I'm scared"
"Mom, my failed Mom, please erase my footprints"
how far did I walk   mom's lips were hanging
from a branch of a ginkgo tree   a timid river, flowing backward
turned to flame   the clock was broken, and the *Malgals* and the *Huns*
danced, singeing their bodies with torches   lightning forked from
the head of my penis, and the darkness that came crashing down was
oppressively heavy

너는 네가 무엇을 흔드는지 모르고

너는 네가 무엇을 흔드는지 모르고
너는 그러나 머물러 흔들려 본 적 없고
돌이켜 보면 피가 되는 말
상처와 낙인을 찾아 고이는 말
지은 罪에서 지을 罪로 너는 끌려가고
또 구름을 생각하면 비로 떨어져
썩은 웅덩이에 고이고 베어 먹어도
베어 먹어도 자라나는 너의 죽음
너의 後光, 너는 썩어 詩가 될 테지만

또 네 몸은 울리고 네가 밟은 땅은 갈라진다
날으는 물고기와 熔岩처럼 가슴 속을
떠돌아 다니는 새들, 한바다에서 서로
몸을 뜯어 먹는 친척들 (슬픔은
기쁨을 잘도 낚아채더라)
또 한 모금의 공기와 한 모금의 물을 들이켜고
너는 네가 되고 네 무덤이 되고

이제 가라, 가서 오래 물을 보고
네 입에서 물이 흘러나오거나
오래 물을 보고 네 가슴이 헤엄치도록
이제 가라, 不穩한 도랑을 따라
豫感을 만들며 흔적을 지우며

you don't know what you're shaking

you don't know what you're shaking
and you've never stayed put to be shaken yourself
when you think back there are words that become blood
words that seek out and settle in your wounds and brandings
you're dragged from the sinning you've done to the sinning you'll do
again   when you think of clouds your death falls as rain
and settles in putrid puddles   I cut and eat it, cut and eat it
but your death continues to grow   though you'll rot
and become a poem, your aura will remain

again   your body tolls, the ground you stand on splits
fish fly, birds wander lava-like inside your chest,
and the family of man, inhabiting the same ocean,
bite off and eat pieces of each other's bodies (how easily
sadness snatches away happiness)
again   you gulp a mouthful of air and a mouthful of water
and become yourself and your grave

go now, gaze long at the water
until it flows from your mouth
or gaze long at the water until you feel the waves in your chest
go now, follow the crooked ditch
erasing your footprints as you feel your way

口話

1
앵도를 먹고 무서운 애를 낳았으면 좋겠어
걸어가는 詩가 되었으면 물구나무 서는
오리가 되었으면 嘔吐하는 발가락이 되었으면
발톱 있는 감자가 되었으면 상냥한 工場이
되었으면 날아가는 맷돌이 되었으면 좋겠어
죽고 싶어도 짓궂은 배가 고프고
끌려다니며 잠드는 그림자, 이맘때 먼 먼 저 별에 술 한잔
  따르고 싶더라 내 그리움으로
별아, 네 미끄럼틀을 만들었으면 좋겠어

2
나는 아침 이슬 李氏 노을에 걸린 참새가
내 엄마 나는 껍질 벗긴 소나무 진물
흘리며 꿈꾸고 있어 한없이 풀밭 위를
달리는 몸뚱이 體位를 바꾸고 싶어 正敎會의
돔을 세우고 싶어 體位를 바꾸고 싶어
느낌표와 송곳이 따라와 노래의 그물에
잡히기 전에 어디 숨고 싶어 體位를 바꾸고
싶어 돋아나는 뾰루지 속에 병든 말이
울고 있어 병든 말을 끌어안고 임신할까 봐
지금은 다만 體位를 바꾸고 싶어

3
모든 게 神秘였다 길에서 오줌 누는 여자아이와
곱추 남자와 電子時計 모든 게 神秘였다 채찍 맞은
말이 길게 울었다 모든게 神秘였다 사람이 사람을
괴롭히고, 그러나 죽지 않을 만큼 짓이겼다
모든 게 神秘였다 사랑의 힘 죽음의 힘 죽은 꽃의 힘
모든 게 神秘였다
삼백 육십 오일 駱駝는 타박거렸다
얼마나 멀리 가야 하나 얼마나 가까이 있어야 하는가

oral tale

1

I'd like to eat cherries and give birth to an outrageous child
to become a walking poem   a duck
standing upside down   a vomiting toe
a potato with toenails   a friendly
factory   a flying millstone   even when I feel like dying
my mischievous stomach gets hungry   a shadow falls asleep while
   being
dragged around   about now I'd like to fill a glass
   with wine for that distant star
from yearning, star, I'd like to build a slide for you

2

I   the morning dew   a sparrow suspended in Mr. Yi's sunset
my mom   I'm dreaming   oozing from me the resin of a pine tree
stripped of its skin   running across the grass
I'd like to shift my body   I'd like to build a dome
for the Orthodox Church   I'd like to shift my body
an awl and an exclamation mark chase me   I'd like to hide
before I'm caught in a net of songs   I'd like to shift
my body   inside a growing pimple a sick horse is
crying   maybe I should hug the sick horse and get pregnant
for now I just want to shift my body

3

all was mystery   a little girl peeing in the street
a hunchback and a digital clock   all was mystery   a whipped
horse let out a long cry   all was mystery   one person made
another suffer, crushed him—but not to death
all was mystery   the power of love, the power of death, the power of
dead flowers   all was mystery
for three hundred sixty-five days a camel plodded along
how far do I have to go   how close do I have to stay

(continued)

口話

4
그날 아침 내게는 돈이 있었고 햇빛도
아버지도 있었는데 그날 아침 버드나무는
늘어진 팔로 무언가를 움켜잡지 못하고
그 밤이 토해 낸 아침 나는 울고 있었다
그날 아침 거미줄을 타고 大型 트럭이
달려오고 큰 새들이 작은 새의 눈알을
찍어 먹었다 그날 아침 언덕은 다른 언덕을
뛰어넘고 다른 언덕은 또 다른 언덕을 뛰어넘고
병든 말이 앞발을 모아 번쩍, 들었다 그날
아침 배고픈 江이 지평선을 핥고 내 울음은
동전처럼 떨어졌다

5
먼 나라여
地圖가 감춘 나라여 덧없음의 없음이여
뒤집어진 車바퀴가 헛되이, 구르는 힘이여
먼 나라여
오래 보면 먼지나는 길에도 물결이 일고
길 가던 사람이 풀빛으로 변하는, 먼 나라여

6
여섯살도 채 안되어 개구리 헤엄을 배웠어
자꾸만 물 속으로 가라앉았지 깨진 유리병이
웃고 있었어 그래 나는 엄마를 불렀고
물결이 나를 넘어뜨렸지 내 이름을 삼켰어
배꼽이 우렁이처럼 열리고 내 팔을 깨물었어
피리 소리가 . . . . 밀밭에선 죽은 개가 울고
여러 번 낫질해도 안 쓰러지던 그림자 나는
宇宙보다 넓은 房에 갇혀 있었지 간혹

oral tale

4

that morning though I had money, sunlight,
and a father, that morning the willow tree
couldn't with its dangling arms grab anything
that morning, vomited up by the night, I was crying
that morning a large truck came driving by
upon a spiderweb, big birds pecked at and ate
the eyes of little birds   that morning a hill jumped over
another hill which jumped over a third hill and a sick horse put its
front legs together and jerked them up off the ground
that morning a hungry river licked the horizon and my tears
fell like coins

5

a country far away
a country that maps conceal   the nonexistence of meaningfulness
the energy of a wheel uselessly spinning on an upended car
a country far away
where if you look long enough waves rise from the dusty road
and a passer-by takes on the color of grass   a country far away

6

before turning six I learned to swim, frog-fashion
I had been sinking in the water   a broken glass bottle
was smiling   yes I called to mom
and waves knocked me over   they swallowed my name
my navel opened like a mud snail and bit my arm
the sound of a flute . . .   a dead dog howled in a field of wheat
and my shadow, despite the many strokes of a sickle, wouldn't fall   I
was locked in a room larger than space

(continued)

口話

비행기가 삐라를 뿌렸어 양귀비꽃이 食道를
거슬러 올라왔어 입과 肛門 사이 사랑은
交流로 흐르고 미치기 위해 나는 굶었지
순박한 사람들이 날으는 나를 돌로 후려치고
그래 나는 돌과 함께 떨어졌고 그래 나는
汽車에 뛰어 올랐지 그래, 나는 故鄕을 떠났어

oral tale

from time to time an airplane showered political leaflets
a poppy climbed up my windpipe   love flowed like alternating current
between mouth and asshole   I starved myself to go mad
innocent people pelted me with stones while I was flying
yes I fell with the stones and yes I jumped on a train
yes, I deserted my hometown

出埃及

1
오늘 다 외로와하면
내일 씹을 괴로움이 안 남고
내일 마실 그리움이 안 남는다
오늘은 집에 돌아가자 세편의 映畵를 보고
두 명의 주인공이 살해되는 꼴을 보았으니
운좋게 살아남은 그 녀석을 너라 생각하고
집에 돌아가자, 살아 있으니
수줍어 말고 되돌아 취하지 말고 돌아가자
돌아가 싱싱한 떡잎으로 자라나서
훨훨 날아올라 충격도, 마약도 없이
꿈 속에서 한 편 映畵가 되어 펼쳐지자

2
내가 떠나기 전에 길은 제 길을 밟고
사라져 버리고, 길은 마른 오징어처럼
퍼져 있고 돌이켜 술을 마시면
먼저 취해 길바닥에 드러눕는 愛人,

나는 휑한 地下道에서 뜬눈을 새우다가
헛소리하며 찾아오는 東方博士들을
죽일까봐 겁이 난다

이제 집이 없는 사람은 天國에 셋방을 얻어야 하고
사랑받지 못하는 사람은 아직 欲情에 떠는 늙은 子宮으로
    돌아가야 하고
忿怒에 떠는 손에 닿으면 문둥이와 앉은뱅이까지 낫는단다,
    主여

exodus

1

if you consume all your loneliness today
you won't have any pain left to chew on tomorrow
you won't have any longing left to drink tomorrow
as for today, let's go home   you've watched three films
and seen two main characters murdered
so let me think the lucky one who survived is you
and let's go home   you're alive, so
let's not be self-conscious or go off to get drunk but let's go
    home and then fresh as young leaves let's
fly up to the sky   not from drugs, or from the shocks we've had, but
from our dreams let's spin out a movie

2

even before I start off the road, treading on itself,
vanishes   it lies flat like dried squid
I turn back and drink
my girl friend gets drunk first and sprawls on the ground

I'm afraid that having stayed awake all night
in the murk of an underpass I'll kill the Three Wise Men
when they come talking nonsense

now those who don't have homes should rent rooms in heaven
and those who aren't loved should return to old wombs still
    quivering with lust
and even lepers and cripples will be cured if touched by a hand
    that shakes with wrath, my Lord

移 動

草食民族 사내들의 移動, 아이들은
공터에서 놀게 내버려두고, 여자들은
양장점과 미장원과 부엌에 가둬놓고
外蒙古 군사들은 우리를 번호로 불러냈다
53번, 닭의 내장 속으로 54번, 텍스
속으로 55번, 槍 끝으로 당장 떠나라
이 땅은 어제 재벌급 인사가 買占했다
네가 오른발 내린 곳은 영화배우의 땅
네가 오줌 갈긴 곳은 권투 선수의 情婦의 동생의 땅
밤새 귀뚜라미가 울던 곳은 藝術院 회원의 땅
네 그림자는 두고 가라, 자유로운 잡초들에게
잡념도 던져주어라, 거수 경례하라
정욕의 재를 날리며 꼬리표를 달고 출근하는
바람에게, 풀 먹인 날개를 자랑하며
植民地의 首都를 사열하는 새들에게
잘 가꾸어진 가로수는 말발굽 울리며 앞서
간다, 草食民族 사내들의 移動
週刊誌 겉장의 딸아이들은 키스를 던지며
환송하지만, 약속된 불빛이 안 보인다

displacement

the displacement of the men of the plant and grass-eating tribe
not bothering the children playing in the empty lots
and locking up the women inside the dressmakers' shops,
the hairdressers' shops, the kitchens, the Mongol troops called us out
by numbers   number 53, into the guts of a chicken   number 54, into
a condom   number 55, onto the point of a sword   go, right now   this
land was bought as an investment by a corporate tycoon yesterday
where you planted your right foot is owned by a movie star   where
you peed belongs to a sister of a boxer's mistress   where the cricket
chirped all night is the property of a member of the Art Academy   go,
leaving your shadow behind when you leave   toss your fancies to the
weeds that are free   snap a salute, to the wind that scatters the ashes
of lust and goes off to work with labels attached, and to the birds that
flaunt their starched wings as they parade about inspecting the capital
of their colony   the well-cared for sidewalk trees go ahead, galloping,
their hooves ringing   the displacement of the men
of the plant and grass-eating tribe
youthful daughters on the covers of weekly magazines,
blowing kisses, see them off, but there's not a ray of hope

소 풍

1
고통이라 불리는 도시의 근교에서 나는 한 발을 들고
소변 보는 개들을 보았다 진짜 헬리콥터와 자동차 공장과
진짜 어리석음을 보았다 고통이라 불리는 도시의
근교에서 기차를 타고 가며 나는 보았다 장바구니를 든
임신부와 총을 멘 흑인 병사를

              기차 놀이 기차
          놀이 生은 기차 놀이
나는 보았다 벌거벗고 춤추는 사내들과 구슬치는
튀기 아이와 섬세한 텔레비 안테나를

            욕정인가 욕정인가
          때로 지붕을 뚫고 솟는 이것은
고통이라 불리는 도시의 근교에서 나는 영화를 보고
핫도그를 사 먹고 휘파람 불며 왜, 어디론가 갔다
소돔이여, 두꺼워 가는 발바닥이여, 움직이는 성채여

2
나의 代父 하늘이여 오늘 나는 네바 江에 갔었다
나는 보았다 가도가도 끝없는 상점과 인형 같은
여자들, 돈 내고 한번 안아보고 싶었다 나의 代父
하늘이여 오늘 나는 지나가는 아이들 머리칼 속에
꽃씨를 뿌렸다 언젠가, 언젠가 꽃들이 내 이름을
부르며 사방에서 걸어오리라 나의 代父 하늘이여
오늘 나는 가파른 담장과 外製 승용차와 아파트
수위들에게 최면을 걸었다 최면에 걸린 네바 江은
아름다왔다 골목마다 뜬 소문이 자라고 싱싱한 꽃들은

excursion

1

in a suburb of the city named Pain I saw dogs peeing
with one leg lifted   I saw a real helicopter, and a car factory,
and real stupidity   while on a train passing through
a suburb of the city named Pain I saw a pregnant woman
carrying a shopping basket, a Negro soldier with a rifle on his shoulder

                                                playing choo-choo   playing
                                   choo-choo   life is playing choo-choo
I saw men dancing naked, a half-breed child
playing with marbles, filigreed television antennas

                                              is this desire   is this desire
                    this thing that sometimes swells up and penetrates the roof
in a suburb of the city named Pain I watched a film
ate a hot dog   and whistling whhhyy went to somewhere
Sodom, the callouses on the soles of feet, the moving castle

2

my godfather sky, today I went to the Neva River
I saw an endless line of shops, and women like dolls
I wanted to buy them to hold in my arms my godfather sky,
today I scattered flower seeds in the hair of passing children   one day
one day the flowers will come walking from all directions calling
my name   my godfather sky, today I mesmerized the tall keep-out walls,
the foreign cars, the doormen of the posh apartment blocks
the mesmerized Neva River was beautiful   rumors grew in every street
and fresh flowers gave off a rotten odor

(continued)

소 풍

썩은 냄새를 풍겼다 최면에 걸린 네바 江은 아름다왔다
잘 빗은 愛人들의 눈찌검, 쑹알거림, 입술 빠는
소리 (불쌍한 내 겨드랑이, 간지러워라) 나의
代父 하늘이여 나는 삯마차를 집어타고 해장국 집에
들어갔다 선지 같은 記憶들을 씹었다, 뱉았다 그리고
지붕을 타고 도망쳐야 했다 달아나면서 꿈꾸며 다리
앞에서 檢問당하고 나는 돌아왔지만 내 꿈은 돌아오지
못하고......

excursion

the mesmerized Neva River was beautiful
the hostile glance of shapely lovers chittering and the sound
of their sucking lips (my poor armpits, how they tingle)
my godfather sky, I grabbed a coach and went into a shop that
made soup for hangovers   I chewed on my memories like blood
pudding dumplings, spit them out and had to run away across
the roofs   I was running away and dreaming and at the foot of
the bridge the authorities checked my papers and I came back
but without my dream . . .

물의 나라에서

1
물 속에 잠든 풀잎
한번 발 내리며
영원히 무너지는
물방울
작은 물이 큰 물
만나는 감격
잠깐 번지는
감격
흐르는 물과 내리는 물의
서로 몸 바꾸기

그대가 물의 발이라면 나는 물의 발가락
그대가 물의 鍾이라면 물의 分子와 分子 사이를

헤집고 밀치며 살 부비는 나는 물의 鍾소리
그대가 물의 입이라면 벌어진 물의 입이라면
나는 하늘에 땅을 잇는 물의 울음 오, 그대가 물의
　일그러진 입이라면

2
풀잎 위에 구르는 물방울
풀줄기를 흔드는 물방울
풀밭을 흔드는 물방울
풀밭을 누르는 물방울

　　맨발로 지우면 맨발에
　　맺히는 물방울
　　눈 감으면 마음에
　　구르는 물방울
　　마음 기울면
　　흘러내리는 물방울

in the realm of water

1
in water the grass fell asleep
drops of water
cease to exist
when their feet touch down
the thrill
of tiny bodies of water merging with larger ones
a momentary
thrill
dripping water and flowing water
interpenetrating

if you're the water's feet I'm its toes
if you're the water's bell I'm its sound, worming and muscling in among
    the molecules, rubbing up against their flesh
if you're the water's mouth, the parted mouth of water,
I'm the tears that link heaven to earth   oh, if you're the
    anguished mouth of water

2
drops of water run down the leaves of grass
drops of water stir their stems
drops of water stir the field of grass
drops of water weigh down the field of grass

        when I put down my bare feet
        drops of water are taken by my bare feet
        when I close my eyes
        drops of water roll about in my head
        when I shut my mind
        drops of water slide down

(continued)

물의 나라에서

제 옆의 물방울에 어리는
다른 물방울의 얼굴
제 옆의 물방울에 걸리는
다른 물방울의 목소리

맨발로 지우면
날개 없는 방아깨비
뛰는 연습을 하고
맨발로 지우면
네 눈은 팍,
흩어져 흐르고

3
누가 물 위를 지나가면
물의 목소리
누가 풀잎 흔들면
풀빛 마음 흔들려
누가 거기 있어?
눈초리, 목마른 눈초리

누가 누구를 흔든다
. . . . . . 안개 . . . . . .
누가 나를 흔든다
풀잎 사이
  물방울,
떠 있는

in the realm of water

the face of a drop of water is reflected
in the droplet next to it
the voice of a drop of water is caught
by the droplet next to it

>   when I put down my bare feet
>   a wingless grasshopper
>   practices jumping
>   when I put down my bare feet
>   your eyes pop out
>   and flow in disarray

3
when someone passes over the water
the voice of the water
when someone shakes the grass
the grass-colored mind is shaken
who's there?
the look, a thirsting look

someone is shaking someone
 . . . fog . . .
someone is shaking me
amidst the grass
            drops of water,
floating

돌아오지 않는 江

1

풀밭에서 잠들었어 내 몸이 물새알처럼 부서지고 날개
   없는
꿈이 기어 나왔어 흐린 하늘을 기어 올라갔어 물새의
발자국을 남기며 풀밭에서 눈 떴어 눈 없는 江이 흘러왔어
건너마을이 따라갔어 칭얼대며 피마자와 옥수수가
   자라 나고
플라스틱 칼이 내 몸에 박혔어 나를 버리고 물이 되었어
겨울을 생각하며 얼음이 되었어 그 다음엔 녹기만 하면 돼
깊이 가라앉아 몸 흔들면 돼, 순대처럼 토막토막 끊어져도
소리 안 지르는 快感, 기억 속에는 늙은 鐘지기만
   남겨두는일

2

江가에 누워 있었어 아낙네들 무우밭을 매고 무우꽃은
   하늘로
올라갔어 누워 그림자를 감추었어 땀이 햇볕보다
먼저 흘러도 慾情은 끼룩끼룩 울며 다녔어 손 헹구고 마음
속에서 물새알을 꺼냈어 단단한 물새알 멀리 던져도 깨지지
않았어 떠도는 비누 거품 떠도는 ...... 벌겋게 녹슨 자갈
   採取船으로
트럭이 다가왔어 엉겁결에 트럭은 떠났어 江가에 누워 있었어
미류나무 흔들릴 때마다 하늘은 뒤뚱거렸어 (신기해, 신기해
저 江을 건너고도 죽음에 닿는 것은) 江가에 누워 있었어
목에 힘 빼고 물고기 化石이 되어 갔어

the river never returns

1

I fell asleep in a field of grass   my body cracked like the shell of a water
bird's egg and a wingless dream crawled out   crawling it climbed to
the distant overcast sky, leaving behind a water bird's footprints   in
the grass I opened my eyes   the eyeless river flowed toward me   a
nearby village followed the river   the corn and castor-oil plants grew,
whimpering, and a plastic knife was plunged into my body   I
abandoned myself and became water   thinking of winter I became ice
now all I have to do is melt, sink deep inside the water and shake my body
the pleasure of not screaming, even when my body is sliced like a sausage
holding in memory only the old bell-keeper

2

I was lying at the riverside   farm women were weeding a *mu* farm
the *mu* blossoms rose toward the sky   by lying flat I hid my shadow
sweat oozed from me even before the sun came out and lust
flew back and forth overhead with a honking sound
I rinsed my hands and from my heart extracted a water bird's egg
a hard-shelled egg   though I threw it far away it didn't break
floating soap bubbles . . . floating   a truck approached the machine
that was dredging up gravel, rust-red   from the riverbed   confused,
it left   I was lying at the riverside   whenever the poplars shook
the sky wobbled (how amazing, how amazing that we arrive at death
even after crossing the river)   I was lying on the riverside   I let my
neck go limp and became a fossilized fish

(continued)

돌아오지 않는 江

3

그대 한없이 어두운 江가를 돌아왔어도 그대 病 이름은
　알아내지
못 했네 그대 傷處 밑에는 한 점 불빛도 보이지 않고 죽은
　물고기는
몸 속을 기웃거렸네 그대 제대로 움직이지 않는 입술
　사이로
詩는 물거품처럼 번지고 苦痛은 길가에서 팔리고 있었지
　내일은
主日이야 그대 아현동 正敎會의 히랍 사제를 기억하는지
　내일은
主日이야 하품과 영광을 위해 돼지떼 속으로 다시
　들어가진
않을는지 그대 툇마루는 아직 어지럽고 어머니는 老患을
　사랑하고
있어 그대 飮料水를 마셔두게 별과 糞尿가 또 한번 그대
　披岸으로
흐르게 하게

the river never returns

3

my dear even after walking long by the dark riverside
  I couldn't divine the name of your disease
my dear there was no light beneath your wound and a dead fish
  snooped about inside your body
my dear between your lips that couldn't move well a poem
  spread like ripples in water
and pain was sold in the street   tomorrow is Sunday
my dear do you remember the priest at the Greek Orthodox
  church in Ahyŏn-dong
tomorrow is Sunday   why don't you rejoin the flock of pigs for a
  yawn and glory
my dear your veranda is still a mess and my mother's loving her
  old-age infirmities
my dear for now down your drink   once more let the stars and
excrement flow to your Buddhahood

여 름 산

여름산은 솟아 오른다
熱氣와 金屬의 투명한 옷자락을 끌어 올리며
솟아 오른다 발등에 못 안 박힌 것들은 다 솟아 오른다
　저기
비행기가 수술톱처럼 하늘을 끊어낸다 은빛 날개가
　곤두선다
그 여자는 佛蘭西에 가겠다고 이번 여름엔 꼭
다녀와야겠다고 그 여자는 잠자는 벌레를 밟았다 모르고
밟았다 부서지면서 물 같은 피가 솟아 올랐다 내가 거듭
　밟았다
그 여자는 佛蘭西에 가겠다고

나는 속으로 욕했다
따지고 보면 욕할 이유가 없었다
당신은 남의 가난이 얼마큼 당신과 관계 있다고
　생각합니까
그 여자는 내가 가난한 사람이 아니라고 말했다
당신은 백 사람 중에 하나가 병들어 아프면 당신도
　아프다고 생각합니까
그 여자는 부질없는 말이라고 대답했다

여름산은 솟아 오른다
여름산은 땀 흘리지 않는다 힘쓰지 않는다
여름산 여름산 여름산 우리는 그늘에서 콜라를 마셨다
콜라를 마시며 佛蘭西를 생각하고 울었다 우는 시늉을
　했다
우리는, 시멘트 포를 등에 지고 사다리 오르는 여인들을
　생각하며 울었다
우는 흉내를 냈다 우리는, 바빌론에 묶여 있는 이스라엘
　사람들을 생각하며 울었다 우는 척했다

the summer mountain

the summer mountain rises
dragging along its transparent vestments of heat and metal
it rises   all whose feet are not nailed down rise too
above, like a surgical saw a plane rips the sky   its silver wings
    angled upward

the woman insisted she'd go to France   she'd go this summer
for sure   she stepped on a sleeping bug   not knowing it was there
she stepped on it   as it cracked, liquid like blood shot up   I too
stepped on it   she insisted she would go to France

I felt critical of her
but reflecting on it there was no reason to be critical of her
how much does the poverty of others mean to you?
she said I wasn't poor
if only one in a hundred is sick and in pain, can you also feel the pain?
senseless questions, she said

the summer mountain rises
the summer mountain doesn't sweat   it doesn't exert itself
the summer mountain the summer mountain the summer
    mountain   we drank cola in the shade
as we drank we cried, thinking of France   we pretended to cry
we cried thinking of the working women climbing ladders with
    sacks of cement on their backs
we pretended to cry   we cried thinking of the Israelites in
    captivity in Babylon   we pretended to cry

(continued)

여 름 산

여름산은 솟아 오른다
한숨 쉬지 않고 솟아 오른다 반짝임과 몽롱함을 뿌리며
  솟아 오른다
우리는 손을 잡았다 잡힌 손에서 물 같은 피가 흘렀다
  살려줘요!

여름산은 무겁게 솟아 오른다
솟아 오르지 않는다 솟아 오르는 모습만 보여 준다
여름산 여름산 여름산 먼지, 매연, 악취로 부서지는
여름산 여름산
여름산

the summer mountain

the summer mountain rises
without taking a breath it rises   shattering shadow and light it
   rises
we held each other's hands   blood flowed from our hands   help!

the summer mountain rises ponderously
it doesn't rise   it generates the illusion that it is rising
the summer mountain the summer mountain the summer mountain
   obliterated by dust, exhaust fumes, toxic stench
the summer mountain the summer mountain
the summer mountain

편 지

1

그 여자에게 편지를 쓴다 매일 쓴다
우체부가 가져가지 않는다 내 동생이 보고
구겨 버린다 이웃 사람이 모르고 밟아 버린다
그래도 매일 편지를 쓴다 길 가다 보면
남의 집 담벼락에 붙어 있다 버드나무 가지
사이에 끼여 있다 아이들이 비행기를 접어
날린다 그래도 매일 편지를 쓴다 우체부가
가져가지 않는다 가져갈 때도 있다 한잔 먹다가
꺼내서 낭독한다 그리운 당신 . . . . . . 빌어먹을,
오늘 나는 결정적으로 편지를 쓴다

2

안녕
오늘 안으로 나는 記憶을 버릴 거요
오늘 안으로 당신을 만나야 해요 왜 그런지
알아요? 내가 뭘 할 수 있다고 믿기 때문이요
나는 선생이 될 거요 될 거라고 믿어요 사실, 나는
아무것도 가르칠 게 없소 내가 가르치면 세상이
속아요 창피하오 그리고 건강하지 못하오 결혼할 수 없소
결혼할 거라고 믿어요

안녕
오늘 안으로
당신을 만나야 해요
편지 전해 줄 방법이 없소

잘 있지 말아요
그리운 . . . .

a letter

1
I write to her   every day I write
the postman doesn't take the letter   my sister notices it
she crumples it   not noticing it my neighbor steps on it
still, every day I write a letter   walking along the road
I notice it stuck on somebody's wall or caught
in the branches of a willow tree   kids fold it into a paper plane
and make it fly   still every day I write   the postman
doesn't take the letter   at times he does take it   while having a drink
he opens it and reads it aloud . . .   my dearest,
damn it   today I finally will write a letter

2
hi
before tomorrow I'm going to desert my memory of you
I've got to see you before tomorrow
why?   because I believe I can do something
I'm going to be a teacher   I believe so   as a matter of fact, I have
nothing to teach   if I teach the world will be
defrauded   I'm ashamed and not very healthy   I can't get married   I
do believe I will get married

hi
I've got to see you
before tomorrow
there's no way I can get this letter to you

don't take care
my dear . . .

라라를 위하여

1

지금, 나뭇잎 하나 반쯤 뒤집어지다 바로 눕는 지금에서
   언젠가로 돌아누우며
지금, 물이었던 피가 물로 돌아가길 기다리는 지금 내게로
   들어와 나를 벗으며
지금, 나 몰래 내 손톱을 밀고 있는 그대
손톱 끝에서 밀리는 공기의 저쪽 끝에서 밀리는

그대, 내 목마름이거나 서글픔
가늘게 오르다가 얇게 깔리며 무섭게 타오르는 그대
나는 듣는다, 그대 벗은 어깨를 타고 흘러 떨어지는
   빛다발의 歡呼

잔뜩 물 오른 그대 속삭임

2

어디서 그대는 아름다운 깃털을 얻어 오는가
초록을 생각하면 초록이 몸에 감기는가
분홍을 생각하면 분홍이 몸에 감기는가
무엇이 그대 모가지를 감싸안으며 멋진 마후라가 되는가

날 때부터 이쁜 마음을 몸에 두른 그대는 행복하여라
행복한 부리로 아스팔트를 쪼며 행복한 발바닥으로 제
   똥을 뭉개는 그대는

for Lara

1
now, a leaf turns half-over and then turns back again
you turn from now to some other time
now, you wait for your blood, once water, to turn back to water
now, you come inside me, and slough me off
and now, not letting me notice, you file my fingernails
and are pushed away to the far edge of the air being displaced at
    my fingertips

you, my thirst or my sorrow
you who ascend meagerly and come crashing down, burning
    fearfully
I hear a cry of delight from the radiance that spreads about and
    down your naked shoulders

you whisper, lush with sap

2
where do you get the lovely feathers
when you think of green does green enwrap your body
when you think of pink does pink enwrap your body
and what is it that becomes the chic scarf encircling your neck

you must be happy having from the moment you were born such a
lovely heart to wear   you peck at the asphalt road with a
    happy beak and squash your shit with happy feet

금촌 가는 길

1
집에 敵이 들어올 것 같았다
(집은 地下室, 집은 개구멍)
흰피톨 같은 아이들이 소리 없이 모였다
귀를 쫑긋 세우고 아버지는 문틈을 내다보았다

밥이 타고 있었다
敵은 집이었다

2
地主는 나이가 어렸다
다투어 사람들이 땅을 나누었다
아버지는 땅을 고르고 물을 뿌렸다
아버지는 신발을 벗어부쳤다
아버지의 발목이 흙에 묻혔다 다시 떠올랐다
깨꽃이 웃고 개가 짖었다
아버지의 발목이 깊이 묻혔다
아버지의 얼굴이 푸른 잎사귀처럼 흔들렸다
......어떤 꽃을 보여 주시겠어요, 아버지

3
되새김위까지 다 비워도 남는
투명한 괴로움
병든 개
그리운 나라
색깔을 흘리며 잠자리가 지나가고
얼룩지는 名節옷

a road to Kŭmch'on

1

it seemed that the enemy would enter our house
(our house a basement, our house a dog's burrow)
the children silently clumped together like white blood cells
my dad, his ears cocked, peeped through the door

the rice was burning
the enemy was our house

2

the landlord was young
people quickly divided the land
my dad plowed and watered his plot
he took off his shoes
his foot buried itself to the ankle in the earth and rose again
the sesame blossoms smiled and a dog barked
my dad's ankle was buried deep
his face quivered like green leaves
   . . . what kind of flowers are you going to show me, Dad

3

even after my oxlike stomach empties
the pain, lucid, remains
a sick dog
a homeland nostalgia
a dragon fly passes dripping color
staining our holiday clothes

(continued)

금촌 가는 길

어머니, 제가 너무 크게 부르면
안 나타나는 짐승
어머니, 저의 몸은 잘 흐르다 고인 물
저의 잠은 허허벌판 추운 잠
어머니

4
故鄕을 벗어나면서도 더럽힌 바람과 구름을 만나며
추수 끝난 논밭을 길게 찢으며
울타리 없는 마을에 또 하나의 별을 허락하며

그대 올 때는 내 뒤로 오라
두려워라 그대 그림자, 비루먹은 날들

그대 올 때는 목소리로 오라
두려워라 그대 그림자, 태울 수 없는

5
어떻게 깨어나야 푸른 잎사귀가 될 수 있을까
기어이 흔들리려고 나는 全身이 아팠다

어디서 깨어나야 그대 내 잎사귀를 흔들어 줄까
그대 손 잡으면 그대 얼굴이 지워지고

가슴으로 걷는 길
얼음짱 밑 환한 집들

6
그대 뿔 없는 괴로움으로 연거푸
내 가슴을 박으며
보여 주었지, 꺼져가는 불빛과 마른
진흙의 입맞춤

a road to Kŭmch'on

Mom, if I call it too loud
the beast doesn't appear
Mom, my body flows easily   pooled water
my sleep is a bleak steppe   a cold sleep
Mom

4
even when I leave my hometown I encounter contaminated air
   and clouds
I cut across rice paddies and fields that have been harvested
I bestow a star on another village without fences

when you come, come behind me
how fearsome your shadow   our mange-afflicted days

when you come, come as a voice
how fearsome your shadow   unburnable

5
how do I have to wake up to become a green leaf
my whole body ached desperately   it wanted to be shaken

where do I have to wake up for you to shake my leaf
if I hold your hand your face disappears

in my mind I walk along a road
beneath thick ice, brightly lit houses

6
my dear, with pain that had no horns
you gored my heart again and again
you introduced me to the kiss
of dying light and drying mud

(continued)

금촌 가는 길

그대 뿔 없는 괴로움으로 연거푸
무엇을 박는지 모르고
깨고 나면 나는 늘 비켜 있었지

그대 눈 가리고 이제 날 찾아오면
부딪게 할 테야 내 눈빛으로 그대 실어
저 투명한 壁에, 여러 번 저 壁에

부딪고 부딪고도 무너지지 못해
한없이 내 귀청을 두드리다
어두운 나라 등에 업고 먼 길 갈 때
내 또 한번 그대의 길을 발길질할 테야

7
아주 낮은 音樂으로 대추나무가 흔들리고
갈라진 흙벽에서
아이 울음 소리

길게 부는 바람 한 가닥 끌어안고
내 지금 가면
땡삐가 나를 쏘리라

아프지 않을 때까지
잎 없는 나를 열어 놓고
땡삐 집이 되리라

a road to Kŭmch'on

my dear, you didn't realize what it was you were goring again
and again with pain that had no horns
whenever I awoke I was untouched

my dear, when with eyes covered you come to see me
with my eyes I'll pick you up and smash you
against the transparent wall   many times against that wall

even after being smashed against it many times you still
will not be broken   you drum endlessly against my eardrums
then set off on a long journey, leaving behind a country in darkness
and I again kick the road you've taken

7
the jujube tree sways to a low-pitched music
through a crack in the mud wall
the crying of a child

if I go now
holding tight to a long ribbon of wind
the wasps will sting me

I'll keep my leafless self open
until I'm without pain
I'll become a nest for the wasps

꽃 피는 아버지

1

아버지
만나러 금촌 가는 길에
쓰러진 나무 하나를 보았다 흙을
파고 세우고 묻어 주었는데 뒤돌아보니
또 쓰러져 있다
저놈은 작부처럼 잠만 자나?
아랫도리 하나로 빌어먹다 보니
자꾸 눕고 싶어지는가 보다
나도 자꾸 눕고 싶어졌다
나는 내 잠 속에 나무 하나
눕히고 금촌으로 갔다
아버지는
벌써 파주로 떠났다 한다
조금만 일찍 와도 만났을텐데
나무가 웃으며 말했다 고향 따앙이 여어기이서
몇리이나 되나 몇리나 되나 몇리나되나......
학교 갔다 오는 아이들이 노래 불렀다
내 고향은 파주가 아니야 경북 상주야
나무는 웃고만 있었다
그날 밤
아버지는 쓰러진 나무처럼
집에 돌아왔다 내 머리를 쓰다듬으며
아버지가 말했다
너는 내가 떨어뜨린 가랑잎이야

flowering dad

1

on my way
to Kŭmch'on to see my dad
I saw a tree stretched out on the ground   I dug a hole,
raised the tree and replanted it   but when I looked back
it was down again
like a prostitute, is sleeping all it does?
since its bottom is what it depends on for a living
I guess it often feels like lying down
I too kept wanting to lie down
in my sleep I laid down
a tree and went to Kŭmch'on
my dad,
people told me,
had already left for P'aju
if only you came a bit earlier you could have met him,
the tree said, smiling   how many *li* is my hometown from here
how many *li*   how many *li* . . .
the children sang, coming home from school
my hometown isn't P'aju   it's Sangju, in Kyŏngsangpukdo
the tree just smiled
that night
dad came home
like a toppled tree
stroking my head he said
you're the little leaf I shed
(continued)

꽃 피는 아버지

2
언덕배기 손바닥만한 땅에 아버지는
고추나무를 심었다
밤 깊으면 공사장 인부들이
고추를 따갔다

아버지의 고함 소리는 고추나무 키 위에
머뭇거렸다
모기와 하루살이 같은 것들이
엉켜 붙었다

내버려 두세요 아버지
얼마나 따가겠어요

보름 후 땅 주인이 찾아와, 집을 지어야겠으니
고추를 따가라고 했다

공사장 인부들이 낄낄 웃었다

3
아무 일도 아닌 걸 가지고 아버지는 저리
화가 나실까 아버지는 목이 말랐다 물을
따라드렸다 아버지, 뭐 그런 걸 가지고
자꾸 그러세요 엄마가 말했다 애, 내버려
둬라 본디 그런 양반인데 뭐 아버지는
돌아누워 눈썹까지 이불을 끌어 당겼다

　　　1932년 단밀 보통학교 졸업식
　　　며칠 전 장날 아버지 떡 좀 사먹어요
　　　그냥 가자 가서 저녁 먹자
　　　아버지이 . . . . . . 또! 이젠 너 안 데리고 다닌다
　　　네 월사금도 내야 하고 교복도 사야 하고 . . . . . .

flowering dad

2

on a postage-stamp size piece of land on a hill my dad
had planted peppers
late at night workers from a factory
used to pick the peppers

my dad's shouts hung suspended
just above the peppers
insects like mosquitoes and mayflies
were jumbled together

let the workers be, Dad
how much can they take

fifteen days later the owner of the land came and told us to pick
   all the peppers
he was going to build a new house on the hill, he said

the factory workers snickered

3

why is dad so upset about such
a trivial thing   he was thirsty   I poured some water
and gave it to him   Dad, why do you keep bothering
about such a small thing   let him be, child, mom said
you know he's always been that way   dad lay with his back toward us
and pulled the bed sheet up over his eyebrows

> on a market day in 1932, a few days before the Tanmil
> Primary School graduation   *Dad, let's get some sweet rice cakes*
> let's just go home   we'll have dinner at home
> *Da-addy* . . . again!   I'm not going to take you with me
> any more   I've got to pay for your school, buy your school
> uniform, and . . .

(continued)

꽃 피는 아버지

아버지, 아버지는 굶었다 그해 모심기하던
날 저녁 아버지는 어지러워 밥도 못 잡숫고
그 다음날 새벽 돌아가셨습니다
아버지, 藥 한 첩 못 써보고

아무도 일찍 잠들지 못했다 아버지는 꽃 모종
하고 싶었지만 꽃밭이 없었다 엄마, 어디에
아버지를 옮겨 심어야 할까요 살아 온 날들
물결 심하게 이는 오늘, 오늘

4
아버지가 회사를 그만두기 며칠 전부터 벌레가 나왕
　　책장을 갉아먹고
있었다 처음엔 두 군데, 다음엔 다섯 군데 쬐그만 홈을
　　파고
고운 톱밥 같은 것을 쏟아냈다 저도 먹어야 살지, 청소할
　　때마다
마른걸레로 훔쳐냈다 아버지는 회사를 그만두고 집에만
　　계셨다
텔레비 앞에서 프로가 끝날 때까지 담배만 피우셨다
　　벌레들은
더 많은 구멍을 파고 고운 나무 가루를 쏟아냈다 보자 누가
　　이기나,
구멍마다 접착제로 틀어막았다 아버지는 낮잠을 주무시다
　　지겨우면
하릴없이, 자전거를 차고 수색에 다녀오시고 어머니가
　　한숨 쉬었다
그만 하세요 어머니, 이젠 연세도 많으시고 . . . . . . 어머니는
　　먼 산을 바라보며
또 한주일이 지나고 나는 보았다 전에 구멍 뚫린 나무
　　뒷편으로
새 구멍이 여러 개 뚫리고 노오란 나무 가루가 무더기,
　　무더기
쌓여 있었다 닦아내도, 닦아내도 노오랗게 묻어났다
　　숟가락을 지우며

flowering dad

dad, he skipped meals that year, one evening
during rice planting he was too dizzy to eat
and the next day early in the morning he died
dad, he didn't even have a chance to take any medicine,
and . . .

nobody could fall asleep early dad had wanted to plant
flowers but there was no flower garden Mom, where
shall I transplant dad the days we've lived
are churning about like waves today, today

4
a few days before my dad quit his job at the company bugs
    began chewing
the lauan bookshelf first in a couple of spots, then in five spots
    they made tiny holes
and left behind what looked like sawdust we should
    understand that even they need food to live on
whenever I cleaned the house I wiped the bookshelf with a dry
    rag after quitting his job
my dad stayed home all day he just smoked cigarettes in front
    of the TV until all the programs finished
the bugs made more holes and dug out more sawdust let's see
    who's going to win
I plugged every hole with glue my dad took naps, and when he
    got bored, for no particular purpose
he'd ride his bicycle to Susaek and my mom sighed come on,
    Mom, you know he's getting old . . .
as she was staring at the distant mountain another week passed,
    and I saw behind the holes I plugged new holes,
and piles and piles of the yellow sawdust I wiped the bookshelf
    over and over again,
and always there was sawdust on the rag putting down a spoon

(continued)

꽃 피는 아버지

어머니가 말했다 창틀에 문턱에 식탁에까지 구멍이 . . . .
　약이 없다는데,
아버지는 밥을, 소처럼, 오래오래 씹고 계셨다

flowering dad

mom said there are more holes in the window frame, the door-
   step, the dining table, and . . . people say there's no cure for it . . .
my dad chewed his rice for a long, long time, like an ox

어떤 싸움의 記錄

그는 아버지의 다리를 잡고 개새끼 건방진 자식 하며
비틀거리며 아버지의 샤쓰를 찢어발기고 아버지는 주먹을
휘둘러 그의 얼굴을 내리쳤지만 나는 보고만 있었다
그는 또 눈알을 부라리며 이 씨발놈아 비겁한 놈아 하며
아버지의 팔을 꺾었고 아버지는 겨우 그의 모가지를
문밖으로 밀쳐냈다 나는 보고만 있었다 그는 신발 신은 채
마루로 다시 기어 올라 술병을 치켜들고 아버지를 내리
찍으려 할 때 어머니와 큰누나와 작은누나의 비명,
나는 앞으로 걸어나갔다 그의 땀 냄새와 술 냄새를 맡으며
그를 똑바로 쳐다보면서 소리 질렀다 죽여 버릴 테야
法도 모르는 놈 나는 개처럼 울부짖었다 죽여 버릴 테야
별은 안 보이고 갸웃이 열린 문 틈으로 사람들의 얼굴이
라일락꽃처럼 반짝였다 나는 또 한번 소리 질렀다
이 동네는 法도 없는 동네냐 法도 없어 法도 그러나
나의 팔은 罪 짓기 싫어 가볍게 떨었다 근처 市場에서
바람이 비린내를 몰아왔다 門 열어두어라 되돌아올
때까지 톡, 톡 물 듣는 소리를 지우며 아버지는 말했다

an account of a fight

holding our dad's leg he cursed at him haughty son of a bitch
he staggered, ripping dad's shirt, and dad flung out his arm
striking him hard in the face with his fist I was just watching
again his eyes flashed, he twisted dad's arm and called him a fucking
coward dad shoved him but couldn't get more than his head out of
the gate I was just watching still wearing shoes he pushed his way
back into the house and picked up a wine bottle he was about to
smash dad with it mom and my first and second sisters screamed
I stepped up to him he reeked of sweat and alcohol I looked
straight at him I'll kill you, I shrieked don't you have any sense
of human decency I yelped like a dog I'll kill you there were
no stars through the narrow space of the open gate, people's faces
shone like lilacs again I shrieked is there no sense of human decency
around here no sense of human decency no human decency my
arms were trembling I was afraid of committing a crime
a gust of wind brought the odor of fish from the nearby market
plip, plop water dripping then dad's voice, cutting through
the silence leave the gate unlocked for when he comes home, he said

家族風景

형은 長子였다 <이 책상에 걸터앉지 마시오—長子白>
형은 서른 한 살 주일마다 聖堂에 나갔다 형은 하나님의
長子였다 聖經을 읽을 때마다 나와 누이들은 형이 기르는
약대였다 어느날 형은 아버지보고 말했다 <저 죽고 싶어요
하란에 가 묻히고 싶어요> 안될 줄 뻔히 알면서도 형은
우겼다 우겼지만 형은 제일 먼저 익은 보리싹이었다 나와
누이들은 모래 바람 속에 먹이 찾아 날아다녔고 어느 날 또
형은 말했다 <아버지 이제 다시는 祭祀를 지내지
않겠어요 좋아요 다시는 안 돌아와요> 그날 나는 울었다
어머니는 형의 와이셔츠를 잡아 당기고 단추가 뚝뚝
떨어졌다 누이들, 떨어지며 빙그르르 돌던 재미 혹시
기억하시는지 그래도 형은 長子였다 아버지와 어머니는
형의 아들 딸이었고 누이들, 그대 産婆들 슬픈 노래를
불렀더랬지 그래도 형은 長子였다 하란에서 멀고 먼
우리집 매일 아침 食卓에 오르던 누이들, 말린 물고기들
혹시 기억하시는지 형은 찢긴 와이셔츠처럼 웃고 있었다

a family scene

our brother was the first son   "don't lean on this desk—written by the
    first son"
he was thirty-one   every Sunday he went to the Catholic church
he was God's first son   whenever he read the Bible, my sisters and I
became the sheep he was shepherding   one day he said to our father
    "I want to die
I want to be buried in Haran" he insisted, though he surely knew
that wasn't possible he insisted, and he was the first barley to ripen
my sisters and I flew about in the wind-whipped sand foraging for food
and on another day our brother said "Dad, I won't worship our ancestors
anymore   all right then, I'll never come back again"   that day I cried
mother grabbed his shirt, the buttons popped   my sisters, do you happen
to remember the fun we had watching the buttons spin as they fell
still, our brother was the first son   our father and mother were his son
and daughter my sisters, you midwives, you sang a sad song, didn't you
still, our brother was the first son   our house far far away from Haran
do you happen to remember the dried fish, my sisters, that appeared
    on our breakfast table every morning
our brother was smiling like a torn shirt

모래내·1978년

1
하늘 한 곳에서 어머니는 늘 아팠다
밤 이슥하도록 전화하고 깨자마자
누이는 또 전화했다 婚姻날이 멀지 않은 거다
눈 감으면 노란 꽃들이 머리 끝까지 흔들리고
時間을 모래 언덕처럼 흘러내렸다
아, 잤다 잠 속에서 다시 잤다
보았다, 달려드는, 눈 속으로, 트럭, 거대한

무서워요 어머니
—애야, 나는 아프단다

2
어제는 먼지 않은 기왓장에
하늘색을 칠하고
오늘 저녁 누이의 결혼 얘기를 듣는다
꿈 속인 듯 멀리 화곡동 불빛이
흔들린다 꿈 속인 듯 아득히 汽笛이 울고
웃음 소리에 놀란 그림자 벽에 춤춘다

노새야, 노새야 빨리 오렴
어린 날의 내가 스물 여덟 살의 나를 끌고 간다
산 넘고 물 건너 간다 노새야, 멀리 가야 해

Moraenae · 1978

1

in one corner of the sky my mother was always sick my sister,
 after speaking on the phone with her fiancé until late in the evening,
called him again as soon as she awoke in the morning
her wedding day is not far off whenever I closed my eyes yellow flowers
quivered above my head and time slid down like sand down a dune
ah, I slept in my sleep I slept again
I saw, hurtling toward my eyes, a huge truck

I'm scared, Mom
—child, I'm sick

2

yesterday I painted the dusty roof tiles
a sky-blue
this evening I hear about my sister's wedding
as in a dream the distant lights from Hwagok-dong
are blinking as in a dream, the dying wail of a train's whistle
a shadow, surprised by laughter, dances on the wall

little mule, little mule come quickly
a child, I lead my twenty-eight-year-old self over the mountain,
across the water little mule, you should go far away

(continued)

모래내·1978년

3

거기서 너는 살았다 선량한 아버지와
볏짚단 같은 어머니, 티밥같이 웃는 누이와 함께
거기서 너는 살았다 기차 소리 목에 걸고
흔들리는 무우꽃 꺾어 깡통에 꽂고 오래 너는 살았다
더 살 수 없는 곳에 사는 사람들을 생각하며
우연히 스치는 질문---새는 어떻게 집을 짓는가
뒹구는 돌은 언제 잠 깨는가 풀잎도 잠을 자는가,
대답하지 못했지만 너는 거기서 살았다 붉게 물들어
담벽을 타고 오르며 동네 아이들 노래 속에 가라앉으며
그리고 어느날 너는 집을 비워 줘야 했다 트럭이
오고 세간을 싣고 여러번 너는 뒤돌아 보아야 했다

Moraenae • 1978

3

you lived there with a simple father, a mother like a bale of rice straw,
a sister with a smile like popped kernels of rice   you lived there
stringing the sounds of trains around your neck, picking
the quivering *mu* flowers to put in tin cans   you lived there a long time
as you thought about people living where it's no longer possible for them
to live questions arose in your head—how do birds build their nests
when does a rolling stone awaken   does grass sleep   though you
couldn't come up with answers, you lived there   like the leaves of red ivy
you climbed the wall, and sank in the songs of the village kids
one day your family had to empty the house   a truck came by
and carted all away   you had to look back many times

벽제

벽제. 목욕탕과 工場 굴뚝. 시외버스 정류장 앞, 중학생과
　아이 업은 여자.
벽제. 가보진 않았지만 훤히 아는 곳. 우리 어버지 하루종일
　사무를 보는 곳.
벽제, 외무부에 다니던 내 친구 일찌기 죽어 그곳에 갔을
　때 다른 친구 하나는
화장장 事務長. 모두 깜짝 놀랐더라는 뒷얘기. 내가 첫휴가
　나왔을 때 학교에서
만난 그 녀석. 몰라보게 키가 크고 살이 붙어 물어봤더니
　<글쎄, 몸이 자꾸
좋아지는구나>하던 그 녀석. 무던히 꼿꼿해 시험 보면
　面接에서 떨어지곤 하던
녀석. 큰누님은 시집 가고 어린 동생들, 흔들리던 살림에도
　공부 잘하다가
腎臟炎. 그날, 비 오던 날 친구들 모여 한줌한줌 뼈를 뿌릴
　때 <진달래 꽃 옆에
뿌려주면 좋아하지 않을까> 친구들, 흙이 되기 전에 또 비
　맞는 그 녀석 생각하고,
울음 소리 . . . . . . 벽제. 오늘 아침 우리집 집수리 하는 사
　내, 리 아버지 벽제 皮革工場에
다니신다니까 <벽제가 우리 고향이예요. 아저씨한테 잘
　말씀드려 우리 아이 취직 좀
시켜 주세요. 가죽 공장은 힘든다던데 . . . . . . > 그리운 고향
　벽제. 너무 가까우면 생각도

Pyŏkjae

Pyŏkjae. a public bathhouse and factory chimneys. a middle
   school student and a woman carrying a child on her back
   at a stop for buses serving outlying areas.
Pyŏkjae. a place I know very well though I've never been there.
   where my father works in his office all day.
Pyŏkjae. my friend who'd worked in the Ministry of Foreign
   Affairs died young and was taken to the crematorium there
its director was also a friend. I heard later that my other friends
   were shocked by the coincidence. the friend who died—on my first
furlough during military service I came across him at the university.
   he'd gotten so tall and had gained so much weight I almost didn't
recognize him. when I asked how it happened he said "I don't know,
   my body just keeps growing" he was so uncompromising that he
failed job interviews. his eldest sister married, leaving him with
   their younger brothers and sisters, and though he was responsible
for them he continued to be a good student then his
   kidneys failed. that day, it was raining his friends gathered and
were scattering by the handful his powdered bones they said
   "wouldn't he like us to spread him around the azaleas"
they thought about his getting wet even before being returned to
   earth the weeping sound . . . Pyŏkjae. this morning I mentioned
to the guy who came to do some repairs on our house that my father
   worked at a leather factory in Pyŏkjae and he said "Pyŏkjae's my
hometown. please talk to your dad about my son, about finding him a
   job. I heard the work in a leather factory's hard, but . . . " Pyŏkjae. a
hometown to miss. a hometown you don't think about

(continued)

벽제

안 나는 고향. 음식점과 잡화점, 자전거포 간판이 낡은
  나라. 무우꽃이 노랗게
텃밭에 자라나고 비닐 봉지 날으는 길로 개울음 소리
  들려오는.
벽제. 이별하기 어려우면 가보지 말아야 할, 벽제. 끊어진
  다리.

Pyŏkjae

it's so near. Pyŏkjae. a place where the restaurant, grocery store,
   bicycle shop signs are dilapidated, where the *mu* flowers grow
yellow in small vegetable gardens, and the sound of dogs
   howling is heard along the road where plastic bags blow about.
Pyŏkjae. you should not go there if it's difficult for you to say
good-bye. Pyŏkjae. a broken bridge.

세월의 집 앞에서

하늘엔 미류나무들이 숲을 이루었다.
세월의 집. 이파리를 뒤집으며 너는 놀고 있었다.
만날 수 없음. 나의 눈도 뒤집어줄려?

개울엔 물 먹은 풀들이 조금씩, 말라비틀어졌다.
어린 時節을 힘겹게 보낸 사내들도.
無色의 꽃, 절름거리는 방아깨비, 모두 바람의 친척들.

그리고 산 꼭대기엔 매일 저녁
성냥개비만한 사람이 웅크리고 있었다.
날마다. 우리의 記憶 속에 밥도 안 먹고 사는
사내. 아버지일지도 모른다.

그리고 신촌에서 멋적고 착한 여자와의 하룻밤. (그 여자의
    애인은
海軍下士官이었다) 아침. 창을 열면 산, 푸른 어두운
    보드라운
머리칼로 밀고 밀려오던 山, 아래 흰 병원건물을 잘라내며
가로놓인 기차. (어떤 칸은 수북이 石炭이 실리고
어떤 칸은 그냥 물 먹은 검은 입) 우리의 記憶 속에 꼼짝
    않는,
앞머리 없는 기차. 그리고 너의 눈에 물방울처럼
    미끄러지던 세월.

그래 그날, 술을 마시고 어떤 작자를 씹고 씹고 참을 수
    없어
남의 집 꽃밭에 먹은 것을 다 쏟아냈던 날.
내가 부러뜨린 그 약한 꽃들은 어떻게 되었을까.

in front of the house of years

the poplars formed a forest in the sky.
the house of years. you were playing   twirling leaves.
I can't meet you. can you also twirl my eyes?

beside a stream, the grass that drank its water was slowly
    drying out,
as were the men of troubled childhood.
flowers without color, lame locusts, relatives of the wind.

evenings we saw a man no larger than a matchstick
crouching on the mountaintop.
he lives in our memory. he never eats
that man could be our father.

a night with a sweet shy woman in Sinch'on. (her boyfriend
    was a Petty Officer in the navy)   morning.   the mountain outside
the window entered, and stroked her soft and dark blue hair
at the base of the mountain, blocking out the white hospital
    building
a train was stalled. (some cars were loaded with coal, others were
    just dark mouths full of water)   a train without a head,
in our memory it never moves. the years flowed like teardrops
from your eyes.

yes   that day, that day I drank, bitched about some guy,
    got nauseous
and in somebody's flower bed puked up all I'd eaten.
what happened to the delicate flowers I destroyed.

그 날

그날 아버지는 일곱시 기차를 타고 금촌으로 떠났고
여동생은 아홉시에 학교로 갔다 그날 어머니의 낡은
다리는 퉁퉁 부어올랐고 나는 신문사로 가서 하루 종일
노닥거렸다 前方은 무사했고 세상은 완벽했다 없는 것이
없었다 그날 驛前에는 대낮부터 창녀들이 서성거렸고
몇 년 후에 창녀가 될 애들은 집일을 도우거나 어린
동생을 돌보았다 그날 아버지는 未收金 회수 관계로
사장과 다투었고 여동생은 愛人과 함께 음악회에 갔다
그날 퇴근길에 나는 부츠 신은 멋진 여자를 보았고
사람이 사람을 사랑하면 죽일 수도 있을 거라고 생각했다
그날 태연한 나무들 위로 날아 오르는 것은 다 새가
아니었다 나는 보았다 잔디밭 잡초 뽑는 여인들이 자기
삶까지 솎아내는 것을, 집 허무는 사내들이 자기 하늘까지
무너뜨리는 것을 나는 보았다 새占 치는 노인과 便桶의
다정함을 그날 몇 건의 고통사고로 몇 사람이
죽었고 그날 市內 술집과 여관은 여전히 붐볐지만
아무도 그날의 신음 소리를 듣지 못했다
모두 병들었는데 아무도 아프지 않았다

that day

that day my father left for Kŭmch'on on the seven o'clock train
and my younger sister went to school at nine   that day my mother's
worn-out legs swelled like balloons and I went to the newspaper company
and lazed around all day   the border with the North was secure and
all was perfect in the world   nothing was missing   that day
prostitutes hung around the train station from mid-afternoon and girls
who in a few years would become prostitutes helped at home with the
housework or took care of their kid-brothers and sisters   that day
my father had an argument with the president of his company about
collecting a debt for him and my younger sister went to a concert with
her boyfriend   that day on my way home I saw a trim woman in boots
and thought you can even kill someone you love   that day not every-
thing that flew above the indifferent trees was a bird   I saw women
weeding grass, weeding their own lives, and men tearing down houses,
tearing down their own sky   I saw an old fortune-teller with his
fortune-telling bird and the venerable jug he carried for when he had
to pee   that day some people were killed in traffic accidents
and downtown that day the bars and love hotels were crowded as usual
but nobody heard that day's moaning
all were sick but nobody felt the pain

그해 여름이 끝날 무렵

그해 여름이 끝날 무렵 안개는 우리 동네 집들을
가라앉혔다 아득한 곳에서 술 취한 남자들이 누군가를
불러댔고 누구일까, 누구일까 나무들은 설익은 열매를
자꾸 떨어뜨렸다 그해 여름이 끝날 무렵 서리 맞은
친구들은 우수수 떨어지며 결혼했지만 당분간 아이 낳을
생각을 못 했다 거리에는 흰 뼈가 드러난 손가락, 아직
깨꽃이 웃고 있을까 그해 여름이 끝날 무렵 佛蘭西文化院
여직원은 우리에겐 불친절했지만 佛蘭西 사람만 보면
꼬리를 쳤고 꼬리칠 때마다 내 꼬리도 따라 흔들렸다
왜 이래, 언제 마음 편할래? 그래 여름이 끝나고
가을이 와도 아무것도 바뀌지 않았다 어머니는 故鄕에
내려가 땅 부치는 사람의 양식 절반을 合法的으로 강탈
했고 나는 미안했고 미안한 것만으로 나날을
편히 잠들 수 있었다 그해 가을이 깊어갈 때
젓가락만큼 자란 들국화는
내 코를 끌어당겨 죽음의 냄새를 뿜어댔지만
나는 그리 취하지도 않았다 지금 이게 삶이 아니므로,
아니므로 그해 가을이 남겨 놓은 우리는 서로 쳐다봤지만
단단한 물건이었을 뿐이고 같은 하늘을 바라보아도
다른 하늘이 덮치고 겹쳤다
이 조개 껍질은 어떻게 山 위로 올라왔을까?

about the time that summer ended

about the time that summer ended fog swallowed the houses
in our district   somewhere far away drunken men were calling out to
somebody who, who the trees continued dropping
their unripened fruits about the time that summer ended my frost-
nipped friends, falling like the falling leaves, married, but for the time
couldn't consider bringing children into the world   on the streets
white bones showed through fingers   the sesame flowers, will they still
be smiling about the time that summer ended the clerk at the French
Cultural Center was unfriendly toward us, but with people who were
French her tail wagged, and whenever her tail wagged mine did too
what's the problem, when are you finally going to take things easy?
even after that summer ended and autumn began, nothing changed
my mother went to our farm in our hometown and as was her right
took half the tenant's crop   I felt sorry about that, and feeling sorry was
able to sleep well at night   as autumn that year wore on the
chrysanthemums, growing no taller than chopsticks, tugged at my nose
and gave off an odor of death, which didn't get me too drunk,
since what I had then wasn't really a life since it wasn't . . .
after autumn left us we looked at each other and saw only hardness
even when we looked at the sky it was a different sky we each saw
how did this seashell get here on the mountain?

그해 가을

그해 가을 나는 아무에게도 便紙 보내지 않았지만
늙어 軍人 간 친구의 便紙 몇 통을 받았다 세상 나무들은
어김없이 동시에 물들었고 풀빛을 지우며 집들은 언덕을
뻗어나가 하늘에 이르렀다 그해 가을 濟州産 5년생 말은
제 주인에게 대드는 자가용 운전사를 물어뜯었고 어느
유명 작가는 南美紀行文을 연재했다
아버지, 아버지가 여기 계실 줄 몰랐어요
그해 가을 소꿉장난은 國産映畵 보다 시들했으며 길게
하품하는 입은 더 깊고 울창했다 깃발을 올리거나 내릴
때마다 말뚝처럼 사람들은 든든하게 박혔지만 햄머
휘두르는 소리, 들리지 않았다 그해 가을 모래내 앞
샛강에 젊은 뱀장어가 떠오를 때 파헤쳐진 샛강도 둥둥
떠올랐고 高架道路 공사장의 한 사내는 새 깃털과 같은
速度로 떨어져내렸다 그해 가을 개들이 털갈이할 때
지난 여름 번데기 사 먹고 죽은 아이들의 어머니는 후미진
골목길을 서성이고 실성한 늙은이와 天賦의 白痴는
서울역이나 창경원에 버려졌다 그해 가을 한 승려는
人骨로 만든 피리를 불며 密敎僧이 되어 돌아왔고 내가
만날 시간을 정하려 할 때 그 여자는 침을 뱉고 돌아섰다
아버지, 새벽에 나가 꿈 속에 돌아오던 아버지,
여기 묻혀 있을 줄이야

that fall

that fall though I didn't send anybody a letter   I got several from
friends who'd gone off to do the obligatory military service they'd been
postponing   all the trees in the world turned yellow at the same time,
as usual, and houses scaled the hillside right up to the sky, overwhelming
the color of grass   that fall a five-year-old Cheju Island pony bit
somebody's private chauffeur arguing with its owner, and a well-known
writer serialized some travel pieces about his journey to South Africa
Dad, I didn't realize you were going to be here
that fall the children playing house were more tedious even than
Korean films, and the long drawn-out yawns were heavier   whenever we
raised the flag or lowered it people were driven like posts into the ground,
but the sound of a hammer wasn't heard   that fall when a dead
young eel floated to the surface of the stream in front of Moraenae,
the stream, which had been dredged, also floated, and a worker fell
at the speed of a feather from the elevated expressway that was being
built   that fall when dogs changed coats, the mother of the children
who'd died the previous summer after eating sautéed silkworm larvae
bought from a sidewalk vendor, hung out on dark street corners
a senile old man was abandoned at the Seoul train station,
as was a congenital idiot at the Ch'anggyŏng Palace   that fall a
Buddhist monk returned as a mystic, playing a flute made of human
bone, and when I asked a woman for a date she spit and turned away
my father, who used to leave home in the early morning and come back
in my dreams, how would I have known he was buried here

(continued)

그해 가을

그해 가을 나는 세상에서 재미 못 봤다는 투의 말버릇은
버리기로 결심했지만 이 결심도 농담 이상의 것은
아니었다 떨어진 은행잎이나 나둥그러진 매미를 주워
성냥갑 속에 모아두고 나도 누이도 房門을 안으로
잠갔다 그해 가을 나는 어떤 가을도 그해의 것이
아님을 알았으며 아무것도 美化시키지 않기 위해서는
卑下시키지도 않는 法을 배워야 했다
아버지, 아버지! 내가 네 아버지냐
그해 가을 나는 살아온 날들과 살아갈 날들을 다 살아
버렸지만 壁에 맺힌 물방울 같은 또 한 女子를 만났다
그 여자가 흩어지기 전까지 세상 모든 눈들이 감기지
않을 것을 나는 알았고 그래서 그레고르 잠자의 家族들이
移葬을 끝내고 소풍 갈 준비를 하는 것을 이해했다
아버지, 아버지 . . . . . . 씹새끼, 너는 입이 열이라도 말 못해
그해 가을, 假面 뒤의 얼굴은 假面이었다

that fall

that fall I decided to break my habit of talking as though there wasn't
any fun in my life, but even that decision turned out to be no more
than a joke   I picked up fallen ginkgo leaves and dead cicadas and kept
them in match boxes, and my sister and I locked our rooms from inside
that fall I realized there was no fall that belonged to any particular year
and I taught myself not to debase things so as not to beautify them
Dad, Dad!   am I your dad
that fall I lived all the days I'd lived, and those I was going to live
but I met another woman, who was like a drop of water clinging
to a wall, and I realized that not an eye in all the world would close
until she splattered, so I understood why Gregor Samsa's family
prepared to go on an outing after burying him
Dad, Dad . . . you little fucker, you should be too ashamed to talk
that fall, the face behind the mask was a mask

그날 아침 우리들의 팔다리여

그날 아침 비 왔다 개이고 다시 흐리고 갑자기 항아리에서
물이 새고 장독이 깨지고 그날 아침 工具들 실은 트럭이
장사진을 이루고 어떤 녀석은 머리에 흰 띠 두르고 깃발을
흔들고 계집애들 소리내어 껌 씹으며 히히닥거리며 줄 맞춰
가고 버스를 타서나 내려서나 우리는 한결같은 군대 얘기
잠시 침묵. 다시 군대 얘기 <비상 걸리면 높은 양반들도
불나게 뛰었지 . . . . . . > 그날 아침 鐘樓에는 鐘이 없고 종이로
　접은
새들 곤두박질하고 우리는 나직이 군가를 흥얼거렸다 그날
　아침
안개와 뜬소문은 속옷까지 기어들었고 빈터엔 유리 조각이
굽은 쇠못이 벌겋게 녹슨 철근이 파밭에는 장다리가 길가에선
학교 가는 아이가 울면서 그 어머니가 주먹질하며 달려오면서
<이 옘병할 놈아, 네 에미를 잡아먹어라> 그날 아침
테니스 코트에는 날씬한 여자와 건장한 사내가 흰
　유니폼을 입고
흰 모자 흰 운동화를 신고 흰 공을 가볍게 밀어 치고
그날 아침 동네 개들은 물불 안 가리고 올라타고 쫓아도
도망 안 가고 여인숙 門을 밀치며 침 뱉는 작부들 우리는

that morning our arms and our legs

that morning it rained, cleared, and clouded up again
suddenly a jug leaked water, a crock of *toenjang* cracked,
a fleet of trucks ferrying factory workers assembled,
a guy with a white band tied round his forehead wagged a flag,
girls chewing gum and giggling walked along in single file
on the bus and off it we talked of the obligatory military service
we'd done   silence for a moment. talk about the military again
"an emergency, and the top brass were running too, as though
they'd catch fire . . . "   that morning a bell was missing from
a bell tower   origami birds plunged headlong to the ground   with low
voices we hummed a military song   that morning fog and rumors
infiltrated our underwear   on an abandoned lot there were pieces
of glass, a bent nail, a rusted steel rod   on a small farm green onions
went to seed   on a street a child going to school cried, and his mother,
following behind, shook her fist at him   "god damn you,
devour your mother"   that morning at the tennis court a slim woman
and a trim man, in white tennis togs, white caps and white sneakers,
smoothly stroked a white ball   that morning the village dogs
mounted one another with impunity and didn't run off
even when chased   whores leaving their seedy hotels spit at them

(continued)

그날 아침 우리들의 팔다리여

다시 군대 얘기 <휴가 끝나고 돌아올 때 선임하사를
    만났더랬어
그 씨팔놈 . . . . . . > 그날 아침 매일 아침처럼 라디오에선 미국
사람이
<What is this?>라고 물었고 학생들이 따라 대답했다
<홧 이즈 디스?> 그날 아침 헤어지며 우리는 식은 욕망을
피로를 기억 상실을 군대 얘기로 만들었고 대충 즐거웠고
오 그날 아침 우리들의 팔다리여, 무한 창공의 깃발이여

that morning our arms and our legs

again talk of the military "on my way back from leave I ran into our
Chief Petty Officer, that son of a bitch . . ." that morning
like every other morning an American voice on the radio asked
"What is this?" and the students repeated "whu-at i-z di-su?"
that morning as we took leave of each other, from our chilled aspirations,
our fatigue, our faded memories, more talk of the military
we'd had fun, not too much, not too little
oh that morning our arms and our legs, flags in an infinite sky

그러나 어느날 우연히

어느날 갑자기 망치는 못을 박지 못하고 어느날 갑자기
　　벼는 잠들지
못한다 어느날 갑자기 재벌의 아들과 高官의 딸이
　　결혼하고 내 아버지는
예고 없이 해고된다 어느날 갑자기 새는 갓낳은 제 새끼를
　　쪼아먹고
캬바레에서 춤추던 有夫女들 얼굴 가린 채 줄줄이
　　끌려나오고 어느날
갑자기 내 친구들은 考試에 합격하거나 文壇에 데뷔하거나
　　美國으로
발령을 받는다 어느날 갑자기 벽돌을 나르던 조랑말이
　　왼쪽 뒷다리를
삐고 과로한 운전수는 달리는 버스 핸들 앞에서 졸도한다

어느날 갑자기 미류나무는 뿌리채 뽑히고 선생은 생선이
　　되고 아이들은
발랑까지고 어떤 노래는 금지되고 어떤 사람은 수상해지고
　　고양이 새끼는
이빨을 드러낸다 어느날 갑자기 꽃잎은 발톱으로 변하고
　　쳐녀는 養老院으로
가고 엽기 살인범은 불심 검문에서 체포되고 어느날
　　갑자기 괘종시계는
멎고 내 아버지는 오른팔을 못 쓰고 수도꼭지는 헛돈다

however suddenly one day

suddenly one day a hammer can't drive nails and rice plants
    can't fall asleep
suddenly one day the heir to a business empire marries the
    daughter of a high-ranking government official and my father
    is peremptorily fired
suddenly one day a bird pecks at and then eats its just-born
    chicks
a cabaret is raided, married women, hiding their faces,
    are led out
and my friends pass the national exams for aspiring government
    bureaucrats
or they receive official recognition as writers   or they're sent
    to the U.S. by their companies
suddenly one day a small horse carrying bricks sprains its left
    rear leg and an overworked bus driver passes out at the wheel

suddenly one day poplars are uprooted, teachers become fish,
    children are spoiled rotten,
certain songs are banned, certain people become suspects, a
    kitten shows its teeth
suddenly one day flower petals become claws, virgins are shipped
    to homes for old men,
a sadistic killer is arrested by a police patrol and suddenly one
    day a grandfather clock stops, my father can't move his right arm,
    and the knob of the faucet turns but the valve won't open

(continued)

그러나 어느날 우연히

어느날 갑자기 여드름 투성이 소년은 풀 먹인 군복을 입고
   돌아오고
조울증의 사내는 종적을 감추고 어느날 갑자기 일흔이
   넘은 노파의 배에서
돌덩이 같은 胎兒가 꺼내지고 죽은 줄만 알았던 삼촌이
   사할린에서 편지를
보내온다 어느날 갑자기, 갑자기 옆집 아이가 트럭에
   깔리고 축대와 뚝에
금이 가고 月給이 오르고 바짓단이 틀어지고 연꽃이 피고
   갑자기,
한약방 주인은 國會議員이 된다 어느날 갑자기, 갑자기
   장님이 눈을 뜨고
앉은뱅이가 걷고 갑자기, X이 서지 않는다

어느날 갑자기 주민증을 잃고 주소와 생년월일을 까먹고
   갑자기,
왜 사는지 도무지 알 수 없고

그러나 어느날 우연히 풀섶 아래 돌쩌귀를 들치면 얼마나
   많은 불개미들이
꼬물거리며 죽은 지렁이를 갉아 먹고 얼마나 많은 하얀
   개미 알들이 꿈꾸며
흙 한 점 묻지 않고 가지런히 놓여 있는지

however suddenly one day

suddenly one day a pimply-faced boy returns in a starched
   military uniform   a depressed man disappears
a withered lump of fetus is extracted from a woman in her
   seventies   a presumed-dead uncle sends a letter from Sakhalin
suddenly one day, suddenly, a neighborhood child is crushed
   beneath a truck
a wall and a levee crack, salaries are raised, the bottoms of
   trousers fray, lotus flowers bloom
and suddenly the owner of an Oriental-medicine clinic is elected
   to the National Assembly
suddenly one day, suddenly, a blind man can see, a cripple
   walks
 and suddenly my you-know-what won't get hard

suddenly one day I lose my residence card and forget my
   address and date of birth and suddenly
I don't understand why I live

however suddenly one day I lift a rock from the grass and find
   swarms
of squirming red ants chomping at a dead earthworm and there
   are heaps of white ant eggs
laid out neatly   unsullied by soil   dreaming

人生·1978년 11월

1978년 11월 나는 人生이 부르는 소리를 들었다 시내
음식점 곰탕 국물에선 몇 마리의 파리가 건져졌고 안개 속을
지나가는 얼굴들, 몇 개씩 무리지어 지워졌다 어떤 말도
뜻을 가질 만큼 분명하지 않았다 확인할 수 있는 것은
시멘트 바닥을 가르는 햄머 소리 눈썹을 밀어붙인 눈
그림자처럼 떠오르는 舞踊手의 팔 ... ... 술이 머리 끝까지
　올라
왔을 때 새들은 침착하게 떨어져내렸고 그 침묵도 비명도
아닌 순간의 뜨거움 1978년 11월 人生은 추수 끝난
갯밭의 목소리로 나를 불렀다 울음이 끝난 뒤 끈끈한
힘을 모아 나는 대답했다 ... ... 뒤처진 철새의 날갯짓으로

life • November 1978

in November 1978 I heard life calling me   at a downtown
restaurant flies were fished from a pot of soup   faces passing
in the fog disappeared, a few at a time, their words too faint
to be understood   all I was aware of for sure was the clatter of a
jackhammer ripping up the concrete floor, eyes with shaved eyebrows,
a dancer's arms wafting upward, shadow-like . . . .   as the *soju* surged to
the top of my head, birds fell serenely down   the heat of the moment
neither silence nor shriek   in November 1978 life called to me in the
voice of a mudflat farm after harvest   when I finished crying I mustered
up my sluggish strength and answered . . .
the frantic winging of a migrating bird that's fallen far behind

성탄절

성탄절 날 나는 하루 종일 코만 풀었다 아무 愛人도
나를 불러주지 않았다 나는 아무에게나 電話했다 집에
없다는 것이었다 아무도 없어요 아무도 없어요 아무도
살지 않으니 죽음도 없어요 내 목소리가 빨간 제라늄처럼
흔들리다가 . . . . . . 나는 아무 데도 살지 않는 愛人이 보고
싶었다 그 여자의 눈 묻은 구두가 보고 싶었다 성탄절 날
나는 낮잠을 두 번 잤다 한 번은 그여자의 옷을 벗겼다
싫어요 안돼요 한 번은 그 여자의 알몸을 파묻고 있었다
흙이 떨어질 때마다 그 여자는 깔깔 웃었다 멀고 먼
성탄절 나는 Pavese의 詩를 읽었다 1950년 Pavese
自殺, 1950년? 어디서 그를 만났던가 그의 詩는
정말 좋았다 죽을 정도로 좋으니 죽을 수밖에 성탄절 날
Pavese는 내 품에서 천천히 죽어갔다 나는 살아 있었지만
지겨웠고 지겨웠고 아무 데도 살지 않는 愛人이 보고
　싶었다
키스! 그 여자가 내 목덜미 여러 군데 입술 자국을
남겨 주길 . . . Pavese는 내 품에서 천천히 죽어 갔다 나는
그의 故鄕 튜린의 娼女였고 그가 죽어 간 下宿房이었다
　나는
살아 있었고 그는 죽어 갔다 아무도 태어나지 않았다

Christmas

on Christmas I blew my nose all day   no girl friend called
I telephoned anybody   I was told she wasn't home
nobody is   nobody is   since nobody lives there is no death
my voice was wavering like a red geranium. . .   I longed to see
my girl friend who didn't live anywhere   I longed to see her shoes
powdered with snow   on Christmas I took two naps   during one
I was peeling off her clothes   ooh no, I don't want to   oh no,
you shouldn't   during the other I was burying her naked body
at each spadeful of dirt she laughed with pleasure   on Christmas long
long ago I read Pavese's poems   in 1950 he killed himself   1950?
where did I come across him   his poems were really good
he had to kill himself since his poems were too good   on Christmas
Pavese was dying slowly in my arms   I was alive but I was bored
I was bored and I longed to see my girl friend who didn't live anywhere
a kiss!   I wished she'd leave the mark of her lips all over my neck . . .
Pavese was dying slowly in my arms   I was a prostitute in his hometown
of Turin, I was the room in the boarding house where he died
I was alive and he was dying   nobody was born

蒙昧日記

1

한 時代의 여물은 苦痛과 한 時代의
신발인 絶望感 너는 날으는 물이요
웃는 물이요 너는 表現할 수 없었다
한 時代의 非行과 한 時代의 不感症을
한 時代의 길가에서 너는 사랑의 편지를
주웠지만 아무에게도 傳하지 않았다
너는 死亡했다 그리고 먹고 마셨다
한 時代의 습기와 한 時代의 노린내를
너는 두 개의 입으로 토해냈다 자고 나면
햇볕에 이불을 말리고 떠벌려 입을 말리고
시들어갔다

2

처음엔 물건이 사라지고 다음엔
물건에 대한 記憶이 사라지고
한 世代가 오고 또 한 世代가 간다
처음엔 비 맞은 성냥이 안 켜지고 다음엔
비 맞은 해바라기가 빛난다 끔찍하다
비 맞은 공포여, 웃음과 신음의 華燭

어떻든 살아야겠다는 마음이 어떻든
살 수 없다는 마음을 업고 발바닥이
땅을 업고 그림자가 實物을 업고 쓰레기가
밥상을 업고 입이 자꾸만, 肛門을 빨고

天國은 유곽의 窓이요 뜨물처럼 오르는
希望, 希望─늙은 권투 선수

a journal of ignorance

1

pain, time's fodder, and depression, its
shoes   you are water that flies
and water that laughs   you couldn't find words
to express the delinquency of the times, its indifference
you came upon a love letter in the street
but didn't deliver it to anyone
you died   you ate and drank   from your two mouths
you excreted the dankness of the times and its stench
on awakening you dried the bed sheet in the sun
to dry your mouth you opened it
and slowly you withered

2

first the object disappears
then the memory of the object disappears
one generation comes as another goes
first a rain-soaked match does not ignite
then a rain-soaked sunflower shines   grotesque
oh rain-soaked fear, a marriage of laughter and a groan

my feeling that I should somehow manage to live carries
the feeling that somehow I won't be able to
my feet carry the ground   a shadow carries its substance
garbage carries a table heavy with food
and a mouth continually sucks an asshole

paradise is a window of a brothel   hope is the clouded
water left from the first washing of rice
hope rises   hope—an old boxer

(continued)

蒙昧日記

처음엔 苦痛이 사라지고 다음엔
苦痛에 대한 記憶이 사라지고
뒤집힌 눈, 잔물결 지는 눈썹, 映畵는
끝났고 다시 시작된다

3
거룩한
거룩한 거룩한
遲延 지루한 사랑
마음이 物質이 될 때까지 견디기
못 견디기
苦痛은 제가 苦痛인 줄 모르고
苦痛은 제가 苦痛인 줄 미처, 모르고
여기는 아님
여기서
기쁨까지 거리, 波動
여기서 죽음까지 거리, 波動
껴안은 사람들 사이의 무한한 거리, 波動
여기는 아님
여기 있으면서 거기 가기
여기 있은면서 거기 안 가기
여기는 아님 거기 가기 거기 안 가기
여기는 아님 피는 강물 소리를 꿈꾸기 달맞이꽃,
노오란 신음 소리를 꿈꾸기
한 苦痛이 다른 苦痛을 부르기
다른 苦痛이 대답하기 대답 안 하기 대답하기
여기는 아님
아님 아님
아님

a journal of ignorance

first pain disappears
then the memory of pain disappears
eyeballs rotating   eyelashes fluttering, like ripples in water
the movie ends   and begins again

3
holy
holy holy
delay   a tedious love
enduring till feeling transmutes to substance
not enduring
pain doesn't know itself as pain
doesn't know itself as pain, not yet
here   no
the distance from here to joy, a flux
the distance from here to death, a flux
the infinite distance between people embracing, a flux
here   no
going there while staying here
not going there while staying here
here   no   going there   not going there
here   no   the blood dreaming the sound of a river,
    an evening primrose . . .
dreaming the yellow sound of a groan
one pain calling to another pain
the other pain responding   not responding   responding
here, no
no   no
no

사랑日記

1

어디로도 갈 수 없고 어디로 가지 않을 수도 없을 때
마음이여, 몸은 늙은 風車, 휘이 돌려 보시지
몸은 녹슬은 기계, 즐거움에 괴로움 섞어
잠을 만드는 기계
몸은 벌집, 苦痛이 들쑤신 벌집
몸은 눈도 코도 없지만 몸을 쏘아보는 蠟銃과
몸을 냄새 맡는 누리의 미친개들

어디로도 갈 수 없고 어디로 가지 않을 수도 없을 때
마음이여, 몸은 낡은 신발, 뒤집어 신고 날아보시지
―當代의 몸값은 신발 값과 같으니
當代의 몸이 헤고 닳아, 참으로 연한 뱃가죽 보이누나

2

한 마리 말을 옭아매는 馬車의 끈은, 끊어지지 않는
馬車의 사랑 馬車의 꿈 사랑한다 가엾은 내 . . . . . .
미끼에 걸린 물고기를 끌어올리는, 가늘은 낚싯줄은
물고기의 가랑, 사랑은 입으로 말하여지고 사랑은 입을
　꿰뚫고
그래, 개를 걷어차는 구둣발은, 구두를 닮은
소가죽의 사랑 픽, 쓰러지며 소가 남긴 사랑

죽은 나무는 자라지 않지만 죽은 나무의괴로움은
　자라고
지금 밀물은 바로 그 썰물이었으며 愛人은
愛人을 닮은 수렁이었고 愛人을 닮은 무딘 칼이었고
　愛人을 닮은 不安이었고

a journal of love

1

when I can't go anywhere nor stay in one place
my dear heart, my body is an old windmill, why don't you whirl
its sails   my body is a rusty machine, a machine that mixes joy
with suffering, generating sleep
my body is a beehive, a beehive riddled with pain
my body has neither eyes nor nose   but a shotgun glares at it
and the world's mad dogs sniff at it

when I can't go anywhere nor stay in one place
my dear heart, my body is an old pair of shoes   why don't you wear
them inside out and try to fly—in these our times a body's not worth
more than a pair of shoes   in these our times bodies are so used up,
bellies worn so smooth and tissue-thin

2

the harness yoking a horse tight to its wagon is the wagon's
unseverable love and its dream   I love you, my poor . . .
the thin line that pulls up a fish caught by the baited hook
is the fish's love   mouths speak of love and are pierced by love
yes, the leather shoe that kicks a dog is the love of the cow that—
splat—keeled over dead, its hide the likeness of a shoe

a dead tree doesn't grow but its suffering does   what flows now
ebbed before   and my love is a likeness of a mudhole
a likeness of a dull knife, a likeness of insecurity

(continued)

사랑日記

그래, 온 몸으로 번지는 梅毒의 사랑
문드러지면서 입술이, 허벅지가 表現하는 아기자기한 사랑
어머니, 저의 밥은 따뜻한 죽음이요 저의 잠은 비좁은
　　壽衣요
어머니 저는 낙타요 바늘이요 聖者요 聖者의 밥그릇이요
　　어머니, 저는

견디어라 애야, 네 꼬리가 생길 때까지 아무도
만나지 마라, 아픈 것들의 아픔으로 네가 갈 때까지
네 혓바닥은 괴로움의 혓바닥이요 네 손바닥은
　　병든나무의 나뭇잎이요

3
어느날 엄마, 내가 아주 배고프고 다리 아파 목마른 논에
벼포기로 섰다면 엄마, 그 소식 멀리서 전해 듣고 맨발로
뛰어오셔 애야 집에 가자 아버지랑 형이랑 너 기다리느라
잠 한숨 못 잔단다 집에 가자 내가 잘못했어 엄마,
　　그러시겠어요?

그러실 테지만 난 못 돌아가요 뿌리가 끊어지면 물을
못 먹어요 엄마, 제 이삭이나 넉넉히 훑어 가시지요

어느 날 엄마, 내 살 길이 아주 가파르고 군데군데
　　끊어지기도 한다면
엄마, 애야 내 등에 업혀라 밥 많이 먹고 건강해야지 너만
　　보면
마음 아프구나 하시며 내 살 길처럼 타박타박
　　걸어가시겠어요?
엄마 걸어가시겠어요? 발굽이 부러지면

a journal of love

yes, it's the love of the syphilis that spreads through my body
a cute sweet love expressed by lips and thighs as they deform
Mom, my bowl of rice is a warm death, and my sleep is a tight
   shroud
Mom, I'm a camel, a needle, a saint, and a saint's rice bowl
   Mom, I'm

be patient, my child   don't associate with anybody
not until your tail emerges, not until you can go with
the pain of things in pain   your tongue is a tongue of
suffering, your palm a leaf of an afflicted tree

3
one day, Mom, if you get news that I'm far from home and very
   hungry and my legs are sore
and like a stalk of rice I'm standing in the middle of a parched
   rice paddy, would you, Mom, without pausing
even to put on your shoes, come running to me and say child,
   let's go home   your dad and your brother, unsleeping,
have been waiting for you   let's go home   I'm sorry   Mom,
   would you say that?

surely you would, but I can't go back   once broken, my roots can't
drink water   Mom, why don't you just reap your fill of my grains

one day, Mom, if the road of my life becomes very steep and at
   times fragmented
Mom, would you say—child, climb on my back   you should eat
   well and be healthy
it pains me whenever I see you—and would you trudge on along the
   road of my life?
Mom, wouldn't you do that?   even if your hooves splintered

(continued)

사랑日記

등으로 기어 날 안고 가시겠지만 엄마, 난 못 가요
내 四肢는 못박혀 고름 흘려요

엄마, 어느 날 저녁 구름을 밀어내며 애야
여기 예루살렘이야 痛哭으로 壁을 만든 나의 안방이야
요단, 잔잔하단다 요단, 지금 건너라, 빨리 하시면

내가 건너겠어요? 어느 게 나룻배인가요? 아니에요
그건 쓰러진 누이예요 엄마, 누이가 아파요

a journal of love

you'd crawl on your back carrying me in your arms   but Mom,
     I can't go with you
my arms and legs are nailed down and ooze pus

Mom, one day, if you push aside the evening clouds and say
child, this is Jerusalem here   it's my bedroom, made of the walls
that wail   the Jordan is calm   the Jordan, cross it now, quickly

do you think I'd cross?   which one is the ferryboat?   no
it's my sister who fell   Mom, it's my sister who's ill

어째서 이런 일이 벌어졌을까

1
내가 나를 구할 수 있을까
詩가 詩를 구할 수 있을까
왼손이 왼손을 부러뜨릴 수 있을까
돌이킬 수 없는 것도 돌이키고 내 아픈 마음은
잘 논다 놀아난다 얼싸
天國은 말 속에 갇힘
天國의 벽과 자물쇠는 말 속에 갇힘
감옥과 죄수와 죄수의 희망은 말 속에 갇힘
말이 말 속에 갇힘, 갇힌 말이 가둔 말과 흘레 붙음, 얼싸

돌이킬 수 없는 것도 돌이키고 내 아픈 마음은
잘 논다 놀아난다 얼싸

2
나는 <덧없이> 지리멸렬한 行動을 수식하기 위하여
내 나름으로 꿈꾼다 <덧없이> 나는 <어느 날>
돌 속에 바람 불고 사냥개가 천사가 되는
<어느 날> 다시 칠해지는 관청의 灰色 담벽
나는 <집요하게> 한번 젖은 것은 다시 적시고
한번 껴안으면 안 떨어지는 나는 <집요하게>

내 詩에는 終止符가 없다
당대의 廢品들을 열거하기 위하여?
나날의 횡설수설을 기록하기 위하여?

언젠가, 언젠가 나는 <부패에 대한 연구>를 완성 못
　하리라

why did this happen

1
can I save myself
can a poem save itself
can the left hand break itself
after taking back what can't be taken back my aching heart
amuses itself it amuses itself well dee dum
paradise is locked up inside words the walls of paradise and its lock
are locked up inside words the prison, the prisoner and his hopes
are locked up inside words words are locked up inside words, the
words that are locked up inside and those that do the locking up
couple with each other, dee dum

after taking back what can't be taken back my aching heart
amuses itself it amuses itself well dee dum

2
embellishing "for no specific purpose" my incoherent behavior
"for no specific purpose" I dream up my own "one day"
a wind blows inside a stone and a hunting dog becomes an angel
and "one day" the grey walls of the government offices are repainted
I "obsessively" wet what is already wet and
once I "obsessively" lock on to something I never let go

there are no periods in my poem
to catalog the wastage of our times?
to record our daily nonsense?

someday, someday I won't be able to complete my "Studies of
    Corruption"

(continued)

어째서 이런 일이 벌어졌을까

3
숟가락은 밥상 위에 잘 놓여 있고 발가락은 발 끝에
얌전히 달려 있고 담뱃재는 재떨이 속에서 미소짓고
기차는 기차답게 기적을 울리고 개는 이따금 개처럼
짖어 개임을 알리고 나는 요를 깔고 드러눕는다 완벽한
허위 완전 범죄 축축한 공포, 어째서 이런 일이 벌어졌을까

(여러 번 흔들어도 깨지 않는 잠, 나는 잠이었다
자면서 고통과 불행의 正當性을 밝혀냈고 反復法과
기다림의 이데올로기를 완성했다 나는 놀고 먹지 않았다
끊임없이 왜 사는지 물었고 끊임없이 희망을 접어 날렸다)

어째서 이런 일이 벌어졌을까 어째서 육교 위에
버섯이 자라고 버섯이 비둘기는 수박 껍데기를 핥는가
어째서 맨발로, 진흙 바닥에, 헝클어진 머리, 몸뻬이
    차림의
젊은 여인은 통곡하는가 어째서 통곡과 어리석음과
부질없음의 表現은 통곡과 어리석음과 부질없음이
아닌가 어째서 시는 貴族的인가 어째서 貴族的이 아닌가

식은 밥, 식은 밥을 깨우지 못하는 호각 소리—

why did this happen

3

spoons are properly placed upon the table, toes are compliantly
attached to the stubs of feet, cigarette ashes smile inside an ashtray
a train whistles like a train, a dog from time to time barks like a dog
to let others know he is a dog, and I spread a mattress on the floor
and lie down   perfect pretense, perfect crime, sodden fear,
    why did this happen

(I was sleep, a sleep that though shaken many times continued
unbroken   while sleeping I came up with a justification for pain and
unhappiness, a technique for repetition, and an ideology for waiting
I didn't just eat and play   I repeatedly questioned why I lived
I repeatedly folded hope and sailed it through the air)

why did this happen   why do mushrooms grow on overpasses
and pigeons shamelessly tongue the rind of watermelons
why does a young woman, barefoot, in peasant clothes, hair all matted,
go wailing in the mud   why isn't the meaning of wail, of stupidity,
of purposelessness simply wail, stupidity, and purposelessness
why is poetry aristocratic   why not aristocratic

cold rice, even the blast of a whistle can't awaken cold rice—

아들에게

아들아 詩를 쓰면서 나는 사랑을 배웠다 폭력이 없는 나라,
그곳에 조금씩 다가갔다 폭력이 없는 나라, 머리카락에
머리카락 눕듯 사람들 어울리는 곳, 아들아 네
　마음속이었다
아들아 詩를 쓰면서 나는 遲鈍의 감칠맛을 알게 되었다
지겹고 지겨운 일이다 가슴이 콩콩 뛰어도 쥐새끼 한 마리
나타나지 않는다 지겹고 지겹고 무덥다 그러나 늦게 오는
　사람이
안 온다는 보장은 없다 늦게 오는 사람이 드디어 오면
나는 그와 함께 네 마음속에 入場할 것이다 발가락마다
싹이 돋을 것이다 손가락마다 이파리 돋을 것이다
　다알리아 球根 같은
내 아들아 네가 내 말을 믿으면 다알리아꽃이 될 것이다
틀림없이 된다 믿음으로 세운 天國을 믿음으로 부술 수도
　있다
믿음으로 안 되는 일은 없다 아들아 詩를 쓰면서 나는
내 나이 또래의 작부들과 작부들의 물수건과 속쓰림을
　만끽하였다
詩로 쓰고 쓰고 쓰고서도 남는 작부들, 물수건, 속쓰림 . . . . . .
사랑은 응시하는 것이다 빈말이라도 따뜻이 말해주는
　것이다 아들아
빈말이 따뜻한 時代가 왔으니 만끽하여라 한 時代의
　어리석음과
또한 時代의 송구스러움을 마셔라 마음껏 마시고 나서
　토하지 마라
아들아 시를 쓰면서 나는 故鄕을 버렸다 꿈엔들 네 故鄕을
　묻지 마라
생각지도 마라 지금은 故鄕 대신 물이 흐르고 故鄕 대신
　재가 뿌려진다

to my son

my son, while writing poetry I learned love   a country without
    violence
I came to it gradually, the country without violence,
where people, my son, get along the way hairs nest among hairs
it was inside your heart, my son, while writing poetry
that I learned to enjoy the exquisite flavor of stupidity
tedious it is   tedious   my heart throbs in expectation but not
    even a mouse shows up
it's tedious, a tedious matter, and very hot   still, you can't be sure
    the one who hasn't come yet won't come
if he does come I'll enter your heart with him   from each toe
    a bud will sprout, from each finger a green leaf
my son, my dahlia bulb, if you believe in what I tell you
    you'll become a dahlia blossom, for sure
a paradise built with faith can be destroyed by faith   there's nothing
    you can't do with faith   my son, while young and writing poetry
I reveled in prostitutes my age, with their wet towels and
    drink-sour stomachs   I wrote and wrote and wrote about them
in my poems, and always there were more of them, prostitutes
    with wet towels and drink-sour stomachs . . .
to love is to gaze at and speak warmly to someone, even if the
    words are hollow, my son
the time has come when meaningless words sound warm   pleasure
    yourself   drink the stupidity and the humiliation of the time
don't throw up afterward   my son, while young and writing poetry
    I deserted my hometown
do not ask me about your hometown   not even in your dreams
    do not even think about it
now, where our hometown was, water flows   where our
    hometown was
ashes are scattered on the ground

(continued)

아들에게

우리는 누구나 性器 끝에서 왔고 칼 끝을 향해 간다
性器로 칼을 찌를 수는 없다 찌르기 전에 한 번 더 깊이
　찔려라
찔리고 나서도 피를 부르지 마라 아들아 길게 찔리고 피 안
　흘리는 순간,
고요한 시, 고요한 사랑을 받아라 네게 준다 받아라

to my son

we all begin from the head of a cock and end up
   on the point of a knife
you can't stab a knife with a cock before attempting to,
   let yourself again be deeply pierced
do not cry out for blood, even after being stabbed my son,
   when you've been stabbed and do not bleed
then a quiet poem, my silent love, I'll give to you take it

밥에 대하여

1

어느 날 밥이 내게 말하길
<<참, 아저씨나 나나 . . . . . .
말꼬리를 흐리며 밥이 말하길
<<중요한 것은 사과 껍질
찢어 버린 편지
욕설과 하품, 그런 것도
아니고 정말 중요한 것은
氷壁을 오르기 전에
밥 먹어 두는 일.

밥아, 언제 너도 배고픈 적 있었니?

2

밥으로 떡을 만든다
밥으로 술을 만든다
밥으로 과자를 만든다
밥으로 사랑을 만든다 愛人은 못 만든다
밥으로 힘을 쓴다 힘쓰고 나면 피로하다
밥으로 피로를 만들고 悲觀主義와 아카데미즘을 만든다
밥으로 빈대와 파렴치와 방범대원과 娼女를 만든다
밥으로 天國과 유곽과 꿈과 화장실을 만든다 피로하다
　　피로하다 심히 피로하다
밥으로 苦痛을 만든다 밥으로 詩를 만든다 밥으로 철새의
　　날개를 만든다 밥으로 오르가슴에 오른다 밥으로 양심
　　가책에 젖는다 밥으로 푸념과 하품을 만든다 세상은 나쁜
　　꿈 나쁜 꿈 나쁜
밥은 나를 먹고 몹쓸 時代를 만들었다 밥은 나를 먹고
　　동정과 눈물과 能辯을 만들었다, 그러나
밥은 希望을 만들지 못할 것이다 밥이 法이기 때문이다
　　밥은 國法이다 오 밥이여, 어머님 젊으실 적　얼굴이여

about rice

1

one day rice says to me
"well, both you and me . . ."
without finishing it says
"what's important is the skin of an apple,
the letter you tore up,
curses, yawns   no, that's
not it   what's really important is eating rice
before you climb the wall of ice."

rice, have you ever been hungry?

2

we make *ttŏk* with rice
we make wine with rice
we make sweets with rice
we make love with rice   but we can't make lovers with rice
we get energy from rice   we use the energy   we get tired
we make fatigue with rice   and pessimism   and academicism
we make bedbugs   blackguards   night watchmen   prostitutes
we make paradise   brothels   dreams   toilets   I'm tired
    I'm tired   I'm so tired
we make pain with rice   we make poems with rice   we make
    wings for migratory birds with rice   we achieve orgasms with
    rice   we abase ourselves with rice   we make grumbles and
    yawns with rice   life is a bad dream   a bad dream   bad
rice ate me and made the time morbid   rice ate me and made
    pity, tears, and eloquence, but
rice won't be able to make hope because rice is the law
    the national law   oh, rice, the face of my mother when
    she was young

세월에 대하여

1

石手의 삶은 돌을 깨뜨리고 채소 장수의 삶은
하루 종일 서 있다 몬티를 닮은 내 친구는
同時上映館에서 죽치더니 또 어디로 갔는지
세월은 갔고 세월은 갈 것이고 이천 년 되는 해
아침 나는 孫子를 볼 것이다 그래 가야지
天國으로 통하는 車들은 바삐 지나가고
가로수는 줄을 잘 맞춘다 저기, 웬 아이가
쥐꼬리를 잡고 빙빙 돌리며 씽긋 웃는다

세월이여, 얼어붙은 날들이여
야근하고 돌아와 환한 날들을 잠자던 누이들이여

2

피로의 물줄기를 타넘다 보면 때로 이마에
뱀딸기꽃이 피어 오르고 그건 대부분
幻影이었고 때로는 정말 형님이 아들을 낳기도
했다 아버지가 으흐허 웃었다 발가벗은
나무에서 또 몇 개의 열매가 떨어졌다 때로는
얼음 깔린 하늘 위로 붉은 말이 연탄을
끌고 갔다 그건 대부분 幻影이었고 정말
허리 꺾인 아이들이 철 지난 고추나무처럼
언덕에 박혀 있기도 했다 정말 去勢된
친구들이 유행가를 부르며 사라져 갔지만
세월은 흩날리지 않았다 세월은 신다 버린 구두
속에서 곤한 잠을 자다 들키기도 하고
때로는 총알 맞은 새처럼 거꾸로 떨어졌다
아버지는 으흐허 웃고만 있었다 피로의 물줄기를
타넘다 보면 때로 나는 높은 새집 위에서
잠시 쉬기도 하였고 그건 대부분 幻影이었다

I Heard Life Calling Me

about time

1

a mason's life is breaking stone and a grocer's life is standing
all day   my friend who looked like Montgomery Clift used to
hang around a third-class double-feature movie house
I don't know what's become of him   time has passed and will
 continue to pass   on the morning of the first day of the year
 two thousand I'll have a grandson   well, I've got to go   the cars
to paradise flash past, the roadside trees stand in straight rows
over there a child   grins, twirling a mouse by its tail

time, frozen days   sisters who after working all night at the factory
slept through sun-bright days

2

as I followed the river of weariness, from time to time on my
forehead a wild strawberry bloomed   most of that was fantasy
in reality from time to time my elder brother sired a son
laughter burbled from my father   again some fruit fell
from a naked tree   from time to time a red horse crossed
the iced-over sky pulling a cartload of *yŏntan* briquettes
most of that was fantasy   in reality some children, bent double,
were rooted on a hill like red-pepper plants left uncollected during
harvest   in reality my emasculated friends disappeared singing
current pop songs   but time did not fly away
it was sometimes found deeply asleep inside a worn abandoned shoe
and from time to time it plummeted upside down
like a shot-gunned bird   laughter burbled from my father
as I followed the river of weariness from time to time I rested
upon a bird's nest high up   most of that was fantasy too

(continued)

세월에 대하여

3
세월은 갔고 아무도 그 어둡고 깊은 노린내 나는
구멍으로부터 돌아오지 못했다 몇 번인가 되돌아온
便紙 해답은 언제나 질문의 殘骸였고 친구들은
태엽 풀린 비행기처럼 고꾸라지곤 했다 너무
피곤해 手淫을 할 수 없을 때 어른거리던
하얀 풀뿌리 얼어붙은 웅덩이 세월은 갔고
매일매일 작부들은 노래 불렀다 스물 세 살,
스물 네 살 나이가 담뱃진에 노랗게 물들 때까지
또 나는 열 한 시만 되면 버스를 집어 탔고

세월은 갔다 봉제 공장 누이들이 밥 먹는 30분 동안
다리미는 세워졌고 어느 예식장에서나 30분마다
신랑 신부는 바뀌어 갔다 세월은 갔다 변색한
백일 사진 華僑들의 공동묘지 싸구려 밥집 빗물
고인 길바닥, 나뭇잎에도 세월은 갔다 한 아이가
세발 자전거를 타고 번잡한 찻길을 가고 있었다
어떤 사람은 불쌍했고 어떤 사람은 불쌍한
사람을 보고 울었다 아무 것도 그 비리고 어지러운
숨 막히는 구멍으로부터 돌아오지 못했다

4
나는 세월이란 말만 들으면 가슴이 아프다
나는 곱게곱게 자라왔고 몇 개의 돌부리 같은
事件들을 제외하면 아무 일도 없었다 중학교
고등학교 그 어려운 修業時代, 욕정과 영웅심과
부끄러움도 쉽게 風化했다 잊어버릴 것도 없는데
세월은 안개처럼, 醉氣처럼 올라온다
웬 들 판 이 이 렇 게 넓 어 지 고
얼마나빨간작은꽃들이지평선끝까지아물거리는가

about time

3

time passed and nobody was able to come back from the deep dark
stinking hole   a letter was returned several times   answers were always
to be found in the debris of questions and friends would give out
like toy airplanes with spent rubber-bands   when I was too tired to
masturbate the white roots of grass in a frozen swamp swam before
my eyes   time passed   the prostitutes sang songs every day, and by the
time they were twenty-three, twenty-four, cigarettes had stained them
yellow   and every night by eleven I caught the bus for home

and time passed   during the half hour the girls at the sewing
factory ate lunch the clothes irons stood cooling and every half hour
in every wedding hall there was another bride and groom
time passed   in an infant's faded hundredth-day photo   in a public
graveyard for Chinese immigrants   in a cheap restaurant   on a road
where rainwater puddled   on leaves   time passed
on a street busy with traffic a child pedaled along on a tricycle
some people were miserable, some who saw them wept
nothing could come back from the asphyxiating malodorous
   dizzying hole

4

my heart aches whenever I hear the word time
I was brought up as a treasured child, and nothing significant
happened to me other than my encountering in my path
a few stones that I got easily past—middle school, high school,
the difficult period of learning, and then lust, and a desire to be heroic,
and feelings of shame   though there's nothing I need to forget,
time rises like a fog, like drunkenness
how   is   it   that   the   field   grows   so   wide
andhowisitthattherearesomanyredflowerswaveringonthehorizon

(continued)

세월에 대하여

그해
자주 눈이 내리고
빨리 흙탕물로 변해갔다
나는 밤이었다 나는 너와 함께
기차를 타고 민둥산을 지나가고 있
었다 이따금 기차가 멎으면 하얀 物體가
어른거렸고 또 기차는 떠났다 ..... 세월은 갔다

어쩌면 이런 일이 있었는지도 모른다

내가
돌아서
출렁거리는
어둠 속으로 빨려들어갈 때
너는 발을 동동 구르며
부서지기 시작했다
아무 소리도
들리지 않았다

(나는 너를 사랑했다
나는 네가 잠자는 두 평 房이었다
人形 몇 개가 같은 표정으로 앉아 있고
액자 속의 敎會에서는 종소리가 들리는 .....
나는 너의 房이었다
네가 바라보는 풀밭이었다
풀밭 옆으로 숨죽여 흐르는 냇물이었다
그리고 나는 아무 것도 아니었다
문득 고개를 떨군 네
마음 같은,
한줌
空氣였다)

I Heard Life Calling Me

about time

that year
snow fell often and
the road turned quickly muddy
I was night, I was on a train with you
passing a bare mountain the train
from time to time stopped, something white
flickered, and the train moved on again . . . time passed

this also might have happened

when I
turned round
and sank into
the rolling darkness
stamping the ground
you began to break apart
not a sound
was heard

(I loved you
I was the two-*p'yŏng* room you were sleeping in
several dolls with the same face sat next to each other
and a bell tolled in the church inside a framed picture . . .
I was your room
I was the grassy field you gazed at
I was the stream that ran quietly alongside the grassy field
and I was nothing
I was
a handful of air,
like your heart
when of a sudden you bow your head)
(continued)

세월에 대하여

세월이라는 말이 어딘가에서 나를 발견할 때마다
하늘이 눈더미처럼 내려앉고 전깃줄 같은 것이
부들부들 떨고 있는 것을 본다 남들처럼
나도 두어 번 戀愛에 실패했고 그저 실패했을
뿐, 그때마다 유행가가 얼마만큼 절실한지
알았고 노는 사람이나 놀리는 사람이나 그리
행복하지 않다는 것을 알아야 했다 세월은
언제나 남보다 앞서 갔고 나는 또 몇 번씩
그 비좁고 습기찬 門間을 지나가야 했다

about time

whenever the word time comes upon me somewhere
I see the sky falling like an avalanche of snow
and something like an electric wire
vibrating   like others
I several times failed at love   each time was only
a failure   I came to understand how touching pop songs
can be and that neither the toyed with
nor the toyers are happy   time always
ran ahead of me and over and over again I had to
pass through a narrow damp space between doors

處 刑

1
눈알은 개구리알처럼 얼굴을 떠다니고
목구멍까지 칼끝이 올라왔다
누가 내 손을 끌어당기면 길게 늘어났다
이젠 도저히 늘어날 수 없다고 생각했을 때
또 쉽게, 쉽게 늘어났다

방바닥에서 개 짖는 소리가 올라왔다
떠나는 거다
어슬렁거리며 하룻밤, 편히 쉴 곳을 찾아
잠은 든든한 天幕이요 나날은 떨어지는 빗방울이니

2
일어나라, 일어나
내 어머니 부르실 때마다
황폐한 무덤을 허물고 나는 일어섰다
누이의 뺨에는 살얼음이 반짝이고
내 노래는 주르르 흘러내리기도 하였다

방마다 치욕은 녹슨 못처럼 박혀 있었다
나는 그곳에 옷이랑 가족 사진을 걸었다
고개 떨구면, 누룽지 같은 記憶들이 일어나고
손 닿지 않는 곳엔 뽀오얀 곰팡이가 슬었다

아침부터 내 신발은 술로 가득차 있었다
아버지,
가능하면 이 잔을 치워주소서 . . . . . .

execution

1

eyeballs like frogs' eggs were awash on my face
inside me the point of a sword was rising up toward my throat
when someone pulled my hands my arms grew long
when I was sure they couldn't stretch further
they grew longer   easily, easily

a dog's bark rose off the floor
that's it   I'm leaving
to walk about, to search for a place to get a good night's rest
sleep's a dependable tent and days are drops of rain, so . . .

2

come on, get up
whenever my mother called me
I sprung up, breaking through my dismal tomb
a film of ice shone on my sister's cheek
and my song dribbled quickly down

shame, like rusty nails, had been hammered into the walls
in every room   I hung my clothes and family photos there
whenever my head drooped memories rose, stiff as the layer of
    charred rice at the bottom of the pot
where my hands didn't reach, ash-white mold grew

from early morning my shoes were filled with drink
Father,
please take this cup away. . . .

(continued)

處刑

3
그러나 방바닥은 패어 있었고
조금씩 빗물이 고였다
家族들은 말을 하는 대신
뚜-뚜-뚜 통화중 신호만 보냈다
나는 기다렸다 이윽고!
붉은 새털을 단 화살이 뒤통수에 꽂혔다
소리없이 눈동자가 돌아눕고
나는 보았다 어두운
內臟 속에서, 연두색 물개 한 마리가
허공을 치켜보는 것을

execution

3
but the floor of the room was broken
and rainwater little by little pooled in the cracks
my family, instead of speaking to me,
sent me a beep-beep beep-beep busy signal
I waited   at last!
a red-feathered arrow pierced the back of my head
my eyeballs, without a sound, rolled over
and I saw, inside black
entrails, a green seal
looking up at the empty sky

눈

1

눈이 온다 더욱 뚜렷해지는 마음의 수레바퀴 자국
아이들은 찍힌 무우처럼 버려져 있고
전봇대는 크리스마스 씰 속으로 걸어 들어간다

눈이 온다 산등성이 허름한 집들은 白旗를 날리고
한 떼의 검은 새들, 집을 찾지 못한다
마음의 수레 바퀴 자국에서 들리는 수레 바퀴 소리

이제 길은 하늘 바깥을 떠돌고
亡者들은 무덤 위로 얼굴을 든다
一치욕이여, 치욕이여 언제 너도 白旗를 날리려나

2

그 겨울 눈은 허벅지까지 쌓였다
窓을 열면 아, 하고 복면한 산들이 솟아 올랐다

잊혀진 祖上들이 일렬로 걸어왔다
끊임없이 그들은 흰 피를 흘렸다

두 손으로 얼굴을 가리면
온 몸에서 전깃줄이 울고, 얼음짱에
아가미를 부딪는 작은 물고기들이 보였다

3

희생자들은 곳곳에 쌓였다
나무 십자가가 너무 부족했다
잘못, 시체를 밟을 때마다 나는
가슴 속에 물고기를 그렸다

snow

1
it snows   the tracks made by the wheels of the cart that carries my
    heart grow more vivid
children are abandoned, like unmarketable *mu*,
and an electric power pole walks into a Christmas seal

it snows   on the hillside white flags fly above the shabby shacks
a flock of blackbirds can't find its home   from the tracks made by the
wheels of the cart that carries my heart comes the sound of the wheels
    of the cart that carries my heart

now the road meanders alongside the sky
the dead raise their faces above their burial mounds
—shame, shame, when will you, too, fly your white flag

2
that winter the snow piled high as my thigh
when I opened the window the mountain, snow-masked,
    soared upward, saying "aah"

forgotten ancestors came marching in a column
continuously shedding white blood

as with both hands I shielded my face,
electric wires hummed in my body, and I could see
small fish flapping their gills beneath the ice

3
victims were piled up here there everywhere
there was a great lack of wooden crosses
whenever by mistake I stepped on a corpse
I drew in my heart a fish

(continued)

눈

희생자들은 곳곳에 녹아 흘렀다
물고기 뼈가 공중에 떠올랐다

아—하고 누가 소리질렀다
또 한 떼의 희생자들이 희생자들 위에 쓰러졌다
사슴 뿔을 단 치욕이 썰매를 끌고 달려갔다
아—하고 뒷산이 대답했다

snow

the victims melted and flowed here there everywhere
the skeleton of a fish rose in the air

aiee—somebody screamed
another bunch of victims fell on top of the victims
shame, wearing the horns of a deer, ran off pulling a sleigh
aiee—the mountain at my back answered

다시, 정든 유곽에서

1
우리는 어디에서 왔나 우리는 누구냐
우리의 하품하는 입은 세상보다 넓고
우리의 저주는 십자가보다 날카롭게 하늘을 찌른다
우리의 행복은 일류 학교 뱃지를 달고 일류 양장점에서
재단되지만 우리의 절망은 지하도 입구에 앉아 동전
떨어질 때마다 굽실거리는 것이니 밤마다
손은 罪를 더듬고 가랑이는 병약한 아이들을 부르며
소리없이 운다 우리는 어디에서 왔나 우리는 누구냐
우리의 후회는 난잡한 술집, 손님들처럼 붐비고
밤마다 우리의 꿈은 얼어붙은 벌판에서 높은 송전탑처럼
떨고 있으니 날들이여, 정처없는 날들이여 쏟아부어라
농담과 환멸의 꺼지지 않는 불덩이를 廢車의 유리창 같은
우리의 입에 말하게 하라 우리가 누구이며 어디에서
　왔는지를

2
철든 그날부터 변은 변소에서 보지만 마음은 늘 변 본 그
　자리를 떠나지 못하고, 명절날 고운
옷 입은 채 뒹굴고 웃고 연애하고 . . . . . .
우리는 정든 마굿간을 떠나지 못하며

무덤 속에 파랑새를 키우고 잡아 먹고
무덤 위에 애들을 태우고 소풍 나간다 빨리 달린다
참 구경 좋다 때때로

스캔들이 터진다 色이 등등한 늙은이가
의붓딸을 犯하고 습기찬 어느 날 밤 新婚夫婦는
연탄 가스로 죽는다 알몸으로, 그 참 구경 좋다

again, in a congenial brothel

1

where did we come from   who are we
our yawning mouths are wider than the world
our curses pierce the sky more sharply than a cross
wearing the badge of the most prestigious university
we fashion our happiness at the most prestigious tailor shop
but our despair squats at the mouth of a pedestrian underpass
and grovels whenever coins fall   every night hands
grope for sin and crotches weep, calling to their sickly children
where did we come from   who are we   our regrets are as thick
as a swarm of customers at a grubby bar   every night our dreams
shiver like tall power poles in frozen fields, so . . .   days, lost days
pour out unquenchable fireballs of jokes and disillusionment
and make our mouths, that are like the windows of junked cars,
tell who we are and where we came from

2

from the time we're housebroken we always do our shitting in
     toilets, but our hearts can never leave those places where we
     shit, and in our handsome holiday clothes
we lounge around, and laugh, and go out dating . . .
we're stuck inside our congenial stable, and

inside our tombs we raise bluebirds, and eat them,
and then outside our tombs we go for a picnic with our children
we drive off fast   now isn't that amusing

from time to time a scandal breaks out   a lascivious old man
rapes his stepdaughter and one clammy night newlyweds die
of monoxide fumes from a *yŏntan* stove   they are found naked
now isn't that amusing

(continued)

다시, 정든 유곽에서

철든 그날부터 변은 변소에서 보지만 마음은 늘 변 본 그
　　자리를 떠나지 못하고, 악에 받친 소년들은
소주병을 깨고 제 팔뚝을 그어도 ......
여전히 꿈에 부푼 식모애들은 때로, 私生兒를 낳지만

언젠가, 언젠가도 정든 마구간에서 한 발자국, 떼어놓기를
　　우리는 겁내며

3
우리는 살아 있다 살아 손가락을 발바닥으로 짓이긴다
우리는 살아 있다 살아 애써 모은 돈을 인기인과
　　모리배들에게 헌납한다
우리의 욕망은 백화점에서 전시되고 고층 빌딩 아래
　　파묻히기도 하며
우리가 죽어도 변함 없는 좌우명 인내! 도대체 어떤 사내가
새와 짐승과 나비를 만들고 남자와 여자를 만들고 제7일에
휴식하는가 새는 왜 울고 짐승은 무얼 믿고 뛰놀며 나비는
어찌 그리 고운 무늬를 자랑하는가 무슨 낙으로 남자는
　　여자를 끌어안고
엉거주춤 죽음을 만드는가 우리는 살아 있다 정다운
　　무덤에서 종소리,
종소리가 들릴 때까지 후회, 후회, 후회의 종소리가 그칠
　　때까지

4
때로 우리는 듣는다 텃밭에서 올라오는
노오란 파의 목소리 때로 우리는 본다
앞서가는 사내의 삐져나온 머리칼 하나가
가리키는 方向을 무슨 소린지 어떻게, 어떻게
하라는 건지 알 수 없지만 안다 우리가
잘못 살고 있음을 때로 눈은 내린다
참회의 전날 밤 무릎까지 쌓이는 표백된 記憶들
이내 질퍼덕거리며 낡은 구두를 적시지만
때로 우리는 그리워한다 힘없는 눈송이의
모질고 앙칼진 이빨을 때로 하염없이 밀리는

again, in a congenial brothel

from the time I was housebroken, I always did my shitting in a
    toilet   my heart can never leave those places where I shit
wild teenagers smash empty *soju* bottles to gash their arms with, but . . .
from time to time young housemaids, swollen still with hopeful
    dreams, give birth to bastards, but . . .

one day, but even on that day we'll be afraid of stepping
    outside our congenial stable, and

3
we're alive   alive we smash our fingers underfoot
we're alive   alive we gift our hard-earned wages to celebrities
    and profiteers
our desires are displayed in department stores, and sometimes
    entombed beneath skyscrapers
patience! will be our steadfast motto until we die
what kind of man is it that creates birds   beasts   butterflies
    a man and a woman   and rests on the seventh day
why do birds sing   what makes animals frolic without worry
    how do butterflies display such exquisite patterns
 for what pleasure do men embrace women and awkwardly
    bring death into life
we're alive, until from our congenial tomb a bell, a bell tolls,
    until that regret . . . regret . . . regret bell tolls no more

4
from time to time we hear the voices of yellowing scallions
rising from a vegetable patch   from time to time we notice
in what direction a tuft of hair on the head of a man
walking in front of us is pointing   we don't understand
what it means, or what, what on earth it's telling us to do
but we do know we're living the wrong way   from time to
time it snows   the night before we repent, the blanched
memories that mound up to our knees soon melt and soak
our worn-out shoes, but from time to time we long for the
pitiless sharp teeth of the fragile flakes of snow

(continued)

다시, 정든 유곽에서

車들은 보여준다 개죽음을 노래하는 지겹고
숨막히는 행진을 밤마다 공장 굴뚝들은
거세고 몽롱한 사랑으로 별길을 가로막지만
안다 우리들 詩의 이미지는 우리만큼 허약함을
안다 알고 있다 아버지 허리를 잡고 새끼들의
손을 쥐고 이 줄이 언제 끝나는지 뭣하러 줄
서는지 모르고 있음을

5
우리가 이길 수 있는 것은 낡은 구두에 묻은 눈 몇 송이
우리가 부를 수 있는 것은 마음 속에 항시 머무는 먹장구름
우리가 예감할 수 있는 것은 더럽힌 핏줄 더럽힌 자식
兵車는 항시 밥상을 에워싸고 떠나지 않고 꿈틀거리는
　　　　　것은, 물결치는 것은
무거운 솜이불 아, 이 겨울 우리가 이길 수 있는 것은
안개 낀 길을 따라 무더기로 지워지는 나무들
우리의 후회는 눈 쌓인 벌판처럼 끝없고 우리의 피로는
죽음에 닿는 江 한 끼도 거름 없이 고통은 우리의 배를
채우고 담뱃불로 지져도, 얼음판에 비벼도 안 꺼지는 욕정
寶石과 香料로 항문을 채우고서 아, 이 겨울 우리가
이길 수 있는 것은 잠깬 뒤의 하품, 물 마신 뒤의 목마름
　　　　　　　　　　　　　　　　갈 수 있을까
　　　　　　　　　　언제는 몸도
　　　　　　　　　　　　　마음도
　　　　　　　　안 아픈　　　나라로
　　　　　　　　　　　　　귓속에
　　　　　복숭아꽃　　　　　피고
　　　　　　　　노래가
　마을이 되는
　　　　나라로

again, in a congenial brothel

from time to time a sickening, suffocating, endless line of cars
goes marching by, singing of a dog-like death   and every night
the smokestacks of factories, in wild and obscure love
mask the passage of the stars   but we know   we know
the images of our poems are as weak as we ourselves
we know   we do know we don't know where
the end of the line is, or why we're standing here hugging
the waists of our fathers and clutching the hands of our children

5

all we can subdue are the few flakes of snow flecked on our
worn-out shoes   all we can summon are the dark clouds that
never leave our hearts   all we can foresee is the humiliation
of our family line, and the humiliation of our children
military vehicles surround our table and never leave
our heavy cotton blanket surges and rolls like ocean waves
ah, this winter, all we can subdue are the clusters of roadside
trees that fade from sight in the fog   our regret is as endless
as a field covered with snow, our fatigue is a river that joins up
with death   never missing mealtime, pain fills our stomachs
and desire can't be checked, not even after being branded by
cigarettes, or rubbed against ice after we've filled our assholes with
gems and perfume   ah, this winter all we can subdue are our yawns
after waking from sleep, and our thirst after drinking water

                                                            can we go
                        someday, to the country
                                          where
                        neither the body   nor the heart aches
                                    where in my ears
                peaches   bloom
                        and a song
becomes
        a village

                                                    (continued)

다시, 정든 유곽에서

                    갈 수 있을까
            어지러움이
                        맑은 물
                                흐르고

        흐르는 물따라
                    不具의 팔다리가
        흐르는 곳으로
                갈 수 있을까
                    죽은 사람도 일어나
        따뜻한 마음 한잔
                권하는 나라로
            아,   갈 수 있을까
    언제는
            몸도
                마음도
                    안 아픈
                        나라로

6
그리고 어느날 첫사랑이 불어닥친다
그리고 어느날 기다리고 기다리던 사람이 온다
무너진 담벽, 늘어진 꿈과 삐죽 솟은 法을
가뿐히 타넘고 온다 아직 눈 덮인 텃밭에는
싱싱한 파가 자라나고 동네 아이들은
지붕 위에 올라가 연을 날린다 땅에 깔린다
노래는 땅에 스민다 그리고 어느날 집들이
하늘로 떠오르고 고운 바람에 실려 우리는
멀리 간다 창가에 서서 빨리 바뀌는
風景을 바라보며 도란도란 이야기한다
상상도 못할 졸렬한 인간들을 그곳에서
만났다고 . . . . . . 그리고 어느날 다시 흙구덩이 속에
추락할 것이다 뱃가죽으로 기어갈 것이다
사랑해, 라고 중얼거리며 서로 모가지를 물어
뜯을 것이다 그리고 어느날 아무 것도 다시는
불어닥치지 않고 기다림만 남아 흐를 것이다

again, in a congenial brothel

                                    can we go
                              to the country
                                          where confusion flows
                                                      like pure water
                        where deformed limbs
                                          are swept along
          by flowing water
                              can we go there
                                                to the country
                    where even the dead arise
                              and offer a glass of warm heart
                  ah,   can we go
      some day
              to the country
                        where neither the body
                                          nor the heart
                                                      aches

6
and one day love strikes us for the first time
and one day the person you've long been waiting for returns
returns nimbly scaling the collapsed walls   the pendant dreams
the sharp overarching laws   in the still snow-covered vegetable patch
fresh green onions grow and village children
climb on roofs and fly kites   their kites lie flat on the ground
their songs seep into the ground   and one day houses
float up to the sky and we go far away, borne by a gentle breeze
standing by a window we watch the fast-changing scenes
and chat quietly together   we say we've met unimaginably
small-minded people there . . .   one day we'll fall again
into an earthen pit   we'll crawl on the bare skin of our bellies
we'll bite each other's necks while muttering I love you
and yet one day nothing will ever happen to us
and only our anticipation will remain and flow

이제는 다만 때 아닌, 때 늦은 사랑에 대하여

이제는 송곳보다 송곳에 찔린 허벅지에 대하여
말라붙은 눈꺼풀과 문드러진 입술에 대하여
정든 유곽의 맑은 아침과 식은 아랫목에 대하여
이제는, 정든 유곽에서 빠져 나올 수 없는 한 발자국을
위하여 질퍽이는 눈길과 하품하는 굴뚝과 구정물에 흐르는
종소리를 위하여 더럽혀진 처녀들과 비명에 간 사내들의
썩어가는 팔과 꾸들꾸들한 눈동자를 위하여 이제는
누이들과 처제들의 꿈꾸는, 물 같은 목소리에 취하여
버려진 조개 껍질의 보라색 무늬와 길바닥에 쓰러진
까치의 암록색 꼬리에 취하여 노래하리라 정든 유곽
어느 잔칫집 어느 상갓집에도 찾아다니며 피어나고
떨어지는 것들의 낮은 신음 소리에 맞추어 녹은 것
구부러진 것 얼어붙은 것 갈라터진 것 나가떨어진 것들
옆에서 한 번, 한 번만 보고 싶음과 만지고 싶음과 살
　부비고 싶음에
관하여 한 번, 한 번만 부여안고 휘이 돌고 싶음에 관하여
이제는 다만 때 아닌, 때 늦은 사랑에 관하여

now only about love that came at the wrong time, too late

now about a thigh pierced by an awl rather than about the awl
about caked-dry eyelids and disfigured lips   about fresh mornings
in the congenial brothel, and the chill, less-heated side of the room
now about that one step that can't be taken so as to leave the congenial
brothel   about the slushy road, the yawning chimney, and the sound of
a bell that flows along with the muddy water   about despoiled virgins
and the rotting arms and dried-out eyeballs of men who died untimely
now drunk on the fluid dreamy voices of older sisters and younger
sisters-in-law, drunk on the purple pattern of an abandoned seashell,
on the blue-green tail of a dead magpie on the road, I'll sing in tune
with the deep moans of all who go to their congenial brothel, to homes
where there are parties, to homes mourning deaths of all who blossom
and collapse   about wanting to see you once, just once more, wanting
to touch you, to mesh our flesh, to be beside what's been melted, bent,
frozen, split open, hurled aside   about wanting to look at you once,
just once   and about wanting to hold you and to whirl around
   holding you in my arms
now only about love that came at the wrong time, too late

POEMS FROM

South Sea, Silk Mountain

序 詩

간이식당에서 저녁을 사 먹었습니다
늦고 헐한 저녁이 옵니다
낯선 바람이 부는 거리는 미끄럽습니다
사랑하는 사람이여, 당신이 맞은편 골목에서
문득 나를 알아볼 때까지
나는 정처 없읍니다

당신이 문득 나를 알아볼 때까지
나는 정처 없읍니다
사방에서 새소리 번쩍이며 흘러내리고
어두워 가며 몸 뒤트는 풀밭,
당신을 부르는 내 목소리
키 큰 미류나무 사이로 잎잎이 춤춥니다

I Heard Life Calling Me

prelude

I ate dinner at a snack bar
evening comes on, laggard and late
an unfamiliar wind slicks smooth the street
my love, until you of a sudden notice me
from where you are across the street
I won't know where I'm going

my love, until you of a sudden notice me
I won't know where I'm going
bird sounds trill brightly all around
and the grass twists dark in the dusk
my voice, calling you,
dances among the rustling leaves of a tall poplar

정적 하나가

정적 하나가 내 가는 길과 들판을 몰아 옵니다 나직하던
　발걸음 소리가 나둥그러지며 패랭이꽃이 피어납니다
　당신을 찾아가는 곳 어디에나 붉은 班點이 돋지요
　거친 호흡과 身熱은 내 것이고요

휘말린 새들과 뿌리뽑힌 나무를 움켜쥐고서 순식간의
　분노를 느끼게 하세요 정적이 나를 피해 갑니다
　달아나는 정적을 내가 입맞춤하게 해 주세요

a stillness

a stillness comes sweeping across the road and the field
    I walk in   where the faint sound of my footsteps ceases
a pink China rose blooms   in each place I look for you a red
    rash erupts   the heavy breathing and the body heat are mine

let me grab the storm-tossed birds and uprooted trees, and feel a
    surge of fury   the stillness evades me   let me kiss it as it
    slips away

당신은 짐승, 별

당신은 짐승, 별, 내 손가락 끝
뜨겁게 타오르는 정적
외로운 사람들이 따 모으는 꽃씨
외로운 사람들의 죽음
순간과 머나먼 곳,
異邦의 말이 고요하게 시작됩니다.

당신의 살갗 밑으로 大地는 흐릅니다
당신이 나타나면 한 개의 물고기 비늘처럼
무지개 그으며 내가 떨어질 테지만,

you are a beast, a star

you are a beast, a star, a stillness
burning hot at my fingertips
the flower seeds that lonely people collect
the death of lonely people
a moment and a remote place,
foreign words begin to be quietly spoken.

the ground flows beneath your skin
when you appear, like a flaked-off fish scale
I'll fall, arching down like a rainbow   however,

테 스

드문드문 잎이 남은 가을 나무 사이에서
婚禮의 옷을 벗어 깔고 여자는 잠을 이루었다

엄청나게 살이 찐 검은 사슴이
바닥 없는 그녀의 잠을 살피고 있었다

Tess

among the autumn trees spattered sparsely with leaves,
a woman shed her bridal gown, and fell asleep upon it

a prodigiously fat black deer
inspected her bottomless sleep

기억에는 평화가 오지 않고

기억에는 평화가 오지 않고 기억의 카타콤에는 공기가
　더럽고 아픈 기억의 아픈, 국수 빼는 기계처럼 튼튼한
　기억의 막국수, 기억의 원형 경기장에는 혀 떨어진
　입과 꼭지 떨어진 젖과......찢긴 기억의 天幕에는 흰
　피가 눈내림, 내리다 그침,억의 따스한 카타콤으로
　갈까요, 갑시다, 가자니까, 기억의 눅눅한 카타콤으로!

no peace in memory

there is no peace in memory   the air's polluted in the
    catacombs of memory, and the noodles of memory are
    strong as the machine that makes the painful noodles of
    painful memory   in the amphitheater of memory, a mouth
    whose tongue fell out, a breast whose nipple fell off . . .
    white blood snows through the torn tent of memory
    and stops   shall we go to the warm catacombs of memory
    let's go   I said let's go, go to the muggy catacombs of
    memory!

세월의 습곡이여, 기억의 단층이여

무엇과도 바꿀 수 없는 날들이 흘러갔다
강이 하늘로 흐를 때,
명절 떡쌀에 햇살이 부서질 때
우리가 아픈 것은 삶이 우리를
사랑하기 때문이다

무엇과도 바꿀 수 없는 날들이 흘러갔다
흐르는 안개가 아마포처럼 몸에 감길 때,
짐 실은 말 뒷다리가 사람 다리보다 아름다울 때
삶이 가엾다면 우린 거기
묶일 수밖에 없다

the folding of time, the dislocation of memory

the days we wouldn't trade for anything have flowed by
when the river flows skyward,
when sunbeams are mashed into the rice for the holiday *ttŏk*,
the reason we're sick is that
life loves us

the days we wouldn't trade for anything have flowed by
when like linen the flowing fog enwraps our bodies,
when the hind legs of a horse, a load on its back, seem more
beautiful than human legs
even if we feel sorry for life we have no choice
but to be tied to it

치욕에 대하여

치욕은 아름답다 지느러미처럼 섬세하고 유연한 그것
　애밴 처녀 눌린 돼지 머리 치욕은 달다 치욕은 따스하다
　눈처럼 녹아도 이내 딴딴해지는 그것 치욕은 새어
　나온다 며칠이나 잠 못 이룬 사내의 움푹 패인 두 눈에서,

아지랭이!
소리없이, 간단없이
그대의 시야를 유린하는
아지랭이! 아지랭이! 아지랭이!

about shame

shame is beautiful   as fine and supple as the fins of fish   as a
   woman pregnant before marrying   as the savor of a morsel
   of pressed pig's head   shame is sweet   shame is warm
   even when like snow it melts it immediately hardens again
   shame leaks from the hollowed eyes of a man unable for
   days to sleep,

haze!
soundless, endless,
bedeviling your vision
haze! haze! haze!

그리고 다시 안개가 내렸다

그리고 다시 안개가 내렸다 이곳에 입에 담지 못할
　일이있었다 사람들은 말을 하는 대신 무릎으로 기어
　먼 길을 갔다 그리고 다시 안개는 사람들의 살빛으로
　빛났고 썩은 전봇대에 푸른 싹이 돋았다 이곳에 입에
　담지 못할 일이 있었어! 가담하지 않아도 창피한 일이
　있었어! 그때부터 사람이 사람을 만나 개울음 소리를
　질렀다
그리고 다시 안개는 사람들을 안방으로 몰아 넣었다
　소근소근 그들은 이야기했다 입을 벌릴 때마다 허연
　거품이 입술을 적시고 다시 목구멍으로 내려갔다
　마주보지 말아야 했다 서로의 눈길이 서로를 밀어 안개
　속에 가라앉혔다 이따금 汽笛이 울리고
　방바닥이 떠올랐다
아, 이곳에 오래 입에 담지 못할 일이 있었다 ......

and again the fog descended

and again the fog descended   something happened here
   too shameful to talk about   instead of talking about it
   people crawled a long way on their knees   and again the
   fog, gleaming with the hue of human flesh, and from
   decaying telephone poles green buds growing   something
   happened here, too shameful to talk about!   shameful even
   for those who did not take part afterward, on meeting,
   people howled like dogs
and again the fog, driving people back to their hearths
   they spoke to each other in subdued voices   when they opened
   their mouths white foam surged to their lips and drained back
   down their throats   they should not have looked at each other
   when they did they immersed each other in the fog   at times a
   train whistled and the floor of the room heaved up
oh, something happened here too shameful to be talked about
   for a long long time . . .

자고 나면 龜甲 같은 치욕이

자고 나면 龜甲 같은 치욕이 등에 새겨졌다 누이를
　빼놓고는 아무도 몰랐다 낮에는 누울 수 없었다 의자에서
　가능한 한, 의자처럼 쪼그리고 세월이 갔다 아버지를 볼
　수 없었고 믿을 수 없었다 그 사이, 벼들은 자라 한꺼번에
　베어졌다
자고 나면 앞뒤로 발가벗은 나무들이 列을 이었다
　오랑캐들이 말 타고 산을 넘어올 것 같았다 귀 기울이면
　누이는 낮게, 낮게 소리쳤다 치욕이야, 오빠, 치욕이야!
　내가 몸 비틀면 누이는 날아가버렸다

조금씩, 가슴 속의 새집을 뜯어내야 했다
세월의 따스함이 손 끝에 묻어났다
자고 나면 새집은 또 가슴 위에 지어졌다

shame, like a tortoise-shell

whenever I awoke, shame, like a tortoise-shell, was etched upon
   my back   only my sister knew what had happened
   I couldn't lie down during the day   trying to be invisible
   I wadded myself into a chair   time passed   I couldn't look at
   our dad, or trust him   meanwhile the rice ripened, and all of
   it was at one stroke harvested
whenever I awoke, naked trees were standing in a row   I felt
   that the northern barbarians, on their horses, were going to fall
   upon us from the other side of the mountains   when I
   listened carefully I could hear my sister's voice, subdued but
   intense   it's a shame, brother, a shame!   whenever I
   squirmed my sister flew away

I had to carefully pry loose the bird's nest inside my chest
my fingertips felt the warmth of a bird's egg
whenever I awoke, inside my chest was another nest

자주 조상들은 울고 있었다

자주 조상들은 울고 있었다 풀뿌리 아래서 울고 있었다
  누이야, 우리가 하늘이라 믿었던 곳은 자갈밭이었지 자주
  조상들은 울고 있었다 자갈밭에 엎어져 울고 있었다
  누이야, 자갈밭 아래 도랑에는 검은 피가 흐르고 앞산
  구릉에선 늙은 軍人들이 참호를 파고 있었지
  무어라, 무어라고 말을 걸면 허공에서 마른 나뭇잎
  서걱이었지 누이야, 자주 조상들은 울고 있었다 마른
  나뭇잎 속에서 울고 있었다

our ancestors were often crying

our ancestors were often crying   they were crying beneath the
roots of the grass   my sister, what we believed to be sky
turned out to be a field of loose gravel   our ancestors were
often crying   lying on their stomachs in the field of loose
gravel they were crying   my sister, black blood was flowing
in the ditch below the field of loose gravel and elderly soldiers
were digging a trench on the slope of the hill in front of us
when we spoke some words, some words to them, dry leaves
rustled in the empty sky   my sister, our ancestors were often
crying   crying among the dry leaves

아득한 것이 빗방울로

아득한 것이 빗방울로 얼굴을 스치다
아득한 것이 또 한번 빗겨 내리며
그곳을 스치다

그래 나도 간다 몸져 누운 사람들 손발을 밟고
머리 타넘어 나도 간다 반지처럼 빛나는 치욕의
긴 긴 사슬 끄을며

개를 만나면 개를 타고 간다 깨벌레를 만나면
깨벌레에 업혀 간다 아득한 것 살던 곳으로 간다
가서, 아득한 치욕 뿌리내릴까

지금은 빗물 고인 길바닥의 그림자로 간다

what was far away falls like raindrops

what was far away falls like raindrops past my face
what was far away again falls like raindrops, brushing my face
and falling past there

all right, I'll go too, stepping on hands and feet of the sick lying
    in their beds
I'll go, stepping over their heads, dragging a long, long chain
of shame that glitters, ringlike

if I meet a dog I'll go riding that dog   if I meet a sesame bug
I'll go straddling the back of that sesame bug   I'll go to where
    that which was far away used to live
when I get there, will the shame that was far away take root

for now I'm going there, a shadow on the road where rainwater
    has pooled

치욕의 끝

치욕이여,
모락모락 김 나는
한 그릇 쌀밥이여,
꿈꾸는 일이 목 조르는 일 같아
우리 떠난 후에 더욱 빛날 철길이여!

an end to shame

oh shame,
a bowl of rice
still steaming,
because dreaming is like strangling yourself
the railroad tracks will glisten all the more after we depart!

약속의 땅

높은 나무 잎새들은 덧없이 떨리고 팻말들은 쓰러져
　있다 아무 일도 약속대로 지켜지지 않았다 늙은 여인들은
　챙 낮은 집에서 울다가 잠이 들고 비린내 나는 아이들은
　여전히 깊은 물가에서 놀고 있다 강한 자들은 여전히
　강하고 약한 자들은 끝없이 피라밋을 쌓고 있다 사기,
　절도, 살인, 사기, 절도, 절도, 살인......

약속의 땅에서 삼 년을 머물다가
이곳에 집을 버린 새들을 따라 멀리 갈 것인가
아무 일도 지켜지지 않은 약속의 땅에서
녹슨 風磬 소리 들린다

the promised land

the leaves of the tall trees flutter without purpose and signs lie
    flat on the ground   nothing that was promised has been done
    the older women, after crying, have fallen asleep under the low
    eaves and the children, smelling of fish, are still playing in the
    deep water   the strong are still strong and the weak are
    endlessly building a pyramid swindle, theft, murder,
    swindle, theft, theft, murder . . .

will I stay in the promised land three years
and then go far away, following the birds that deserted their
    homes here
I hear the rusty wind-chimes of the promised land
where nothing that was promised has been done

강변 바닥에 돋는 풀

강변 바닥에 돋는 풀, 달리는 풀
미끄러지는 풀
사나운 꿈자리가 되고
능선 비탈을 타고 오르는 이름 모를 꽃들
고개 떨구고 힘겨워 조는 날,

길가에 채이는 코흘리개 아이들
시름 없는 놀이에 겨워 먼 데를 쳐다볼 때

온다, 저기 온다
낡은 가구를 고물상에 넘기고
헐값으로 돌아온 네 엄마
빈 방티에 머리 베고 툇마루에 누우면,

부스럼처럼 피어나는 온동네 꽃들
가난의 냄새는 코를 찔렀다

the grass that grows at the bottom of the river

the grass that grows at the bottom of the river, the grass that runs,
the grass that glides
becomes grotesque dreams
the day nameless flowers climbing the ridgelines of the hills
dipped their heads, tired, and fell asleep,

and when the little kids playing in the street, mother's milk still
    on their lips,
tired of their humdrum games paused, and gazed off into the
    distance

look, there, she's coming
and my mother, returning with almost nothing,
having sold pieces of our worn furniture to the junk dealer,
lay down on our narrow wooden porch and rested her head on
    her basket,

flowers bloomed like a rash throughout the village
and the reek of poverty pierced our noses

인형을 업은 한 아이를

인형을 업은 한 아이를 또 한 아이가 업고 갔다 희망
　고물상 옆 희망 목욕탕, 좌판에 떡을 벌여 놓은 여인은
　시름없이 파리를 쫓았다
한 사내가 아이 둘을 데리고 강가로 걸어갔다 물 속에서
　빨리 해가 끓고 비누 거품에 엉킨 물고기가 거친 숨을
　몰아 쉬었다
사내가 먼저 작은 아이를 물 속에 밀어 넣었다 겁에 질린
　큰 아이가 울면서 달아나다가 사내의 손에 잡혀 물
　속으로 떨어졌다
아버지, 거짓말같이, 아버지......

a child carrying a doll on her back

a child passed by carrying on her back a child who on her back
   carried a doll   the Hope Junk Shop, and beside it the Hope
   Public Bath   a woman with *ttŏk* for sale at her street stand
   indifferently brushed away flies
a man walked to the river with his two children   the sun boiled
   quickly in the water and fish, tangled in detergent bubbles,
   gasped for breath
the man pushed the younger child into the water   frightened
   and crying the other child ran away, was caught by the man,
   and thrown into the water
Dad, just like a lie, Dad . . .

다시 봄이 왔다

비탈진 공터 언덕 위 푸른 풀이 덮이고 그 아래 웅덩이 옆
　미류나무 세 그루 갈라진 밑둥에도 푸른 싹이 돋았다
　때로 늙은 나무도 젊고 싶은가 보다
기다리던 것이 오지 않는다는 것은 누구나 안다 누가
　누구를 사랑하고 누가 누구의 목을 껴안 듯이 비틀었는가
　나도 안다 돼지 목 따는 동네의 더디고 나른한 세월
때로 우리는 묻는다 우리의 굽은 등에 푸른 싹이 돋을까
　묻고 또 묻지만 비계처럼 씹히는 달착지근한 혀, 항시
　우리들 삶은 낡은 유리창에 흔들리는 먼지 낀 풍경 같은
　것이었다
흔들리며 보채며 얼핏 잠들기도 하고 그 잠에서 깨일 땐
　솟아오르고 싶었다 세차장 고무 호스의 길길이 날뛰는
　물줄기처럼 갈기갈기 찢어지며 아우성치며 울고 불고
　머리칼 쥐어뜯고 몸부림치면서……
그런 일은 없었다 돼지 목 따는 동네의 더디고 나른한 세월,
　풀잎 아래 엎드려 숨 죽이면 가슴엔 윤기나는
　石灰層이 깊었다

once again spring came

the steep unused hillside was covered with green grass and at
    the bottom, beside the swamp, young green leaves sprouted
    from the base of triple-trunked poplars   I guess there are
    times when an old tree would also like to be young again
everybody knows that what they've been waiting for will not
    come to pass   who loved who   who broke whose neck
    while pretending to embrace   even I'm familiar with the
    slow and languid way time passes in villages where people
    slaughter pigs by slitting throats
sometimes we question   we question again and again whether
    young green leaves will sprout from our bent backs, but we
    chew on our sweet, juicy, porkfat-like tongues   our lives have
    always been like a landscape, hazy from blowing dust, that we
    see as through an old dusty window
I whined, I was rock-a-byed, sometimes I fell asleep and on
    waking longed to shoot upward like the madly rocketing jets
    of water from the rubber hoses at a car wash, screaming, crying,
    gyrating, tearing at my wild hair . . .
that never happened   time passed slow and languid in villages
    where people slaughter pigs by slitting throats   when I lay
    flat on my stomach holding my breath a seam of coal glowed
    deep inside my chest

격렬한 고통도 없이

격렬한 고통도 없이 날이 가고 봄 여름이 가고 저녁이면
　미친 듯이 떨리는 미류나무 잎새들, 꽃 피는 저녁의
　소슬담을 따라가면 흰 벽엔 아이들이 그려놓은 여자와
　남자, 남자의 키는 유난히 크고 여자는 긴 머리에 레이스
　달린 치마 입었다 그 밑엔 빨간 글씨로 <<우리 선생님>>
격렬한 고통도 없이 날이 가고 사람들은 소리 없이 아팠다
　아파트 놀이터 모래밭에서 수십만 년 밀린 잠을 자고
　나면 잡채다발처럼 걸리는 약속된 땅의 삼십 년,
　격렬한 고통도 없이 날이 가고 가슴 조이고 가슴 뛰고
　변두리 행길엔 늙은 할아비가 끄는 木馬가 있었다 어떤
　아이는 빤쓰도 안 입고 올라탔다 올라탄 아이끼리 머리채
　꼬나잡고 악쓰며 울었다
잡채다발보다 미끄러운 약속된 땅의 삼십 년, 가난한
　여인들이 수군거리는 길을 월부 책장수가 지나갔다,
　격렬한 고통도 없이 . . . . . .

even without there being severe pain

even without there being severe pain days passed spring passed
and summer passed   evenings the leaves of the poplars
trembled crazily   when flowers were in bloom, if I walked
alongside a wall in the evening I would come upon a man
and a woman drawn by children on the white face of the wall
he was unusually tall, she had long hair and wore a skirt
trimmed with lace   underneath, written in red, "our teachers"
even without there being severe pain days passed and people
suffered silently   I slept on the sand of a playground inside
an apartment complex, a sleep put off for tens of thousands of
years, and when I awoke, my thirty years in the promised land
were tangled together like noodles in a dish of *chapch'ae*
even without there being severe pain days passed, my chest
tightened, my heart beat fast, and on a street in the outskirts
there was a cart with wooden horses for children to ride,
pulled by an old man   a child not wearing panties climbed up
on a horse   bawling and screaming, the children on the
horses pulled each other's hair
thirty years in the promised land are more slippery than the
noodles in a dish of *chapch'ae*   a salesman selling books
on a monthly installment plan passed through a street
where poor women were gossiping in low voices to one another,
even without there being severe pain . . .

높이 치솟은 소나무 숲이

높이 치솟은 소나무숲이 불안하였다 밤, 하늘의 구름은
　　층층이 띠를 이루고 그 사이 하늘은 무늬 넣은 떡처럼
　　쌓였다 층층이, 하늘에 가면 말이 필요할까 이곳은 말이
　　통하지 않는 곳
이곳은 말이 통하지 않아! 집에 가면 오늘도 아버지 집에
　　낯선 사람들이 찾아온다 그들은 모두 피를 본 사람들이다
　　의로운 자들, 스스로 의롭게 여기는 자들의 입에 피가
　　묻어 있다 의로운 자들의 입에서 피가 웃는다 아버지는
　　그들을 몹시 사랑하신다.
아, 하고 내 입에서 낮은 한숨이 나온다 오늘 밤 그들은
　　시끄러운 예언자를 묶어 나무에 매달 것이다 예언자도
　　그리 믿을 만한 사람은 못 된다 그의 배는 부르고 걱정이
　　없다 아무도 걱정하는 사람은 없고......
소나무 숲은 더욱 불안해진다 달이 소나무 숲으로 밀려
　　가고 물은 움직이지 않는다

the forest of tall pine trees

the forest of tall pine trees was foreboding   night, the clouds
   stacked up layer upon layer, strips of sky in between like a
   layered rice cake   will words be necessary in heaven   here
   words are not understood
words are not understood here!   today at home strangers
   again come to visit our father   all of them have spilled blood
   there is blood on the lips of these righteous people, of these
   people who see themselves as righteous   blood grins on the
   lips of these righteous people   my father loves them very much.
aah, a soft sigh escapes my mouth   tonight they are going to tie
   up the prating prophet and hang him from a tree   you can't
   even depend upon a prophet   his stomach's full   he has no
   worries   nobody's worried . . .
the forest of pine trees looks even more foreboding   the moon's
   been blown toward the forest, and the water is still

희미한 불이 꺼지지는 않았다

거기 꺼지지 않는 불이 있었다 가슴인지 엉덩인지 모를
　부드러운 것이 어른거렸고, 잡힌 손과 손이 풀렸다 다시
　잡히고 꼼짝할 수 없었다 아침인지 저녁인지 분간할 수
　없었고, 크게 소리치거나 고개 떨구면 소리없이
　불려나갔다 다시 돌아오지 않았다 그 자리에 눌러앉아
　밥을 먹고 변을 보았다 지치면 가족이나 옆사람을
　괴롭혔다 쉽게 노여움이 들었고 발 한번 밟아도 불구대천
　원수가 되었다 어떤 녀석은 사촌 누이의 금이빨을 뽑으러
　달려들었다 목을 졸랐다
조금 더 밝아지거나 어두워지기도 했다 조금 더 밝아질 때
　희망이라고 했다 다시 어두워졌을 때 희망은 벽 위에
　처바른 변 자국 같은 것이었다 천장은 땀에 젖었고
　처녀들의 가슴에선 상한 냄새가 났다 까르르, 처녀들이
　웃었다 그리고 다시 어두워졌을 때 사내들은 눈꺼풀이
　내려온 처녀들을 향해 바지를 내렸다 욕정과 욕정 사이,
　영문모를 아이들이 이리 뛰고 저리 뛰었다
희미한 불이 꺼지지는 않았다 아, 꺼졌으면 하고
　중얼거렸다 꺼지지 않았다

the faint light could not be extinguished

there was a faint light that could not be extinguished
    something soft—breasts or buttocks—quivered, and clutched
    hands relaxed and were again clutched we could not tell if
    it was morning or evening not only those who spoke out but
    also those who lowered their heads were soundlessly taken
    away they never came back others stayed on and ate and
    answered nature's calls when bored we harassed our
    families or our neighbors we were easily annoyed and
    made everlasting enemies of others for something as simple as
    having a foot stepped on someone assaulted his cousin to
    tear out her gold tooth he strangled her
sometimes there was more light other times more darkness
    the time of more light we called hope when the dark came
    again hope was no more than a splotch of shit smeared on the
    wall the ceiling was dank from sweat and a rankness seeped
    from the breasts of the virginal girls the virginal girls giggled
    and whenever it got dark men exposed themselves to the
    virginal girls, whose eyelids were lowered innocent children
    gamboled about amid the lust
there was a faint light that could not be extinguished ah, how I
    wish it would be, I muttered it wasn't

신기하다, 신기해, 햇빛 찬연한 밤마다

어째서 산은 삼각형인가 어째서 물은 삼각형으로 흐르지
　않는가 어째서 여자 젖가슴은 두 개뿐이고 어미 개의
　젖가슴은 여덟 개인가 언제부터 젖가슴은 무덤을
　닮았는가 어떻게 한 나무의 꽃들은 같은 색, 같은 무늬를
　가졌는가 어째서 달팽이는 딱딱한 껍질 속에서 소리
　지르지 않고 귤껍질은 주황색으로 빛나며 풀이 죽는가
　귤껍질의 슬픔은 어디서 오는가
어째서 병신들은 바로 걷지 못하고 전봇대는 완강히
　버티고 서 있는가 왜 해가 떠도 밤인가 매일 밤 물오리는
　어디에서 자는가 무슨 수를 써서 조개는 멋진 껍질을
　만드는가 왜 청년들은 月經을 하지 않는가 어째서
　동네 깡패들은 의리에 죽고 의리에 사는가 왜 장님은
　앞을 못 보고 소방서에서는 불이 나지 않는가 불에 타
　죽어가는 새들은 무슨 말을 하는가
왜 술 먹은 사람은 헛소리를 하고 술 안 먹은 사람도
　헛소리를 하는가 매일 밤 돌사자는 무엇을 기다리는가
　언제부터 風向計는 우두커니 땅만 내려다보는가
　어째서 귀여운 아이들의 볼그레한 뺨은 썩었는가 누가
　소녀들의 가랑이를 벌리고 말뚝을 박았는가 언제부터
　창녀들은 같은 길 같은 골목에서 서성거리고 초라한
　사내들은 어떻게 알고 찾아오는가

amazing, how amazing it is, every night of the shining sun

why is the shape of a mountain triangular why doesn't water
    flow in the shape of a triangle why do women have only one
    pair of nipples, and bitches four since when have breasts
    been shaped like burial mounds how is it that a tree's
    blossoms are all of the same color and pattern why don't
    snails rage out against their hard shells, and why does a
    tangerine's skin glow golden as it withers what's the source
    of its sorrow
why can't the lame walk normally and why are electric power
    poles so obstinately erect why is it night even after the sun
    rises where do ducks sleep at night by what means do
    mollusks create such ingenious shells why don't young men
    menstruate why do neighborhood thugs live for friendship
    and die for friendship why can't the blind see and why isn't
    there fire in fire stations what do birds burning to death say
why do people who drink alcohol and also those who don't
    drink alcohol babble nonsense what do statuary stone lions
    wait for every night since when do wind vanes do nothing
    but stare down at the ground why do the pink cheeks of cute
    children decay who spread and rammed a rod up
    between the legs of young girls since when have whores
    been hanging out on the same corners of the same streets and
    how do their shabby johns know where to look for them

(continued)

신기하다, 신기해, 햇빛 찬연한 밤마다

신기하다, 신기해, 햇빛 찬연한 밤마다 惡夢을
    보내주신 그대,
목마름을 다오! 身熱을 다오!

amazing, how amazing it is, every night of the shining sun

amazing, how amazing it is   come, you who sent me
   nightmares every night of the shining sun,
give me more thirst!   give my body more fever!

내 마음아 아직도 기억하니

내 마음아 아직도 기억하니
우리 함께 개를 끌고 玉山에 갈 때
짝짝인 신발 벗어 들고 산을 오르던 사내
내 마음아 너도 보았니 한 쪽 신발 벗어
하늘 높이 던지던 사내 내 마음아 너도 들었니
인플레가 민들레처럼 피던 시절
민들레 꽃씨처럼 가볍던 그의 웃음 소리

우우우, 어디에도 닿지 않는 길 갑자기 넓어지고
우우, 내 마음아 아직도 너는 기억하니

오른손에 맞은 오른뺨이 왼뺨을 그리워하고
머뭇대던 왼손이 오른뺨을 서러워하던 시절
내 마음아 아직도 기억하니 우리 함께 개를 끌고
玉山에 갈 때 민들레 꽃씨처럼 가볍던 그의 웃음 소리
내 마음아 아직도 너는 그리워하니 우리 함께
술에 밥을 말아 먹어도 취하지 않던 시절을

my heart, do you still remember

my heart, do you still remember
when we went to Jade Mountain, taking our dog,
the guy who kicked off his mismatched shoes and carried them
    up the mountain
my heart, did you also see him hurl one of those shoes
high up toward the sky   my heart, did you also hear
his laughter light as dandelion fluff
that was the time inflation, like the dandelions, was blooming

dum di dum, the road that didn't go anywhere suddenly
    widened
di dum. my heart, do you still remember

that was the time the right cheek having been slapped by the right
    hand longed for the left cheek
and the left hand hesitated, feeling sorry for the right cheek
my heart, do you remember when we went to Jade Mountain,
taking our dog, the guy's laughter light as dandelion fluff
my heart, do you still miss that time we ate the rice
we put in the rice wine and didn't get drunk

머잖아 이 욕망도

머잖아 이 욕망도 끊어질 것이다 달그락거리는 기억의
　서랍에 먼지 곱게 쌓일 것이다 名山大川 흐르던 핏물 든
　숨소리에 이끼 끼일 것이다 머잖아, 머잖아 근질거리는
　혀에 곰팡이 슬고 異物 같은 죽음이 흰피톨 곁에 다가올
　것이다.

흰피톨이여
내 죽음 곁에 누울,
흰 바둑돌 같은 누이들이여!

pretty soon this hungering too

pretty soon this hungering too will be cut off   fine dust will
   cover the rattling drawer of memory   moss, blood-stained by
   the water flowing in our noble mountains and rivers, will
   blanket the sounds of breathing   pretty soon, pretty soon my
   itching tongue will grow moldy and alien death will envelop
   my white blood cells

oh white blood cells
my sisters, white *paduk* stones,
who'd lie down beside my death!

또 비가 오면

사랑하는 어머니 비에 젖으신다
사랑하는 어머니 물에 잠기신다
살 속으로 물이 들어가 몸이 불어나도
사랑하는 어머니 微動도 않으신다
빗물이 눈 속 깊은 곳을 적시고
귓속으로 들어가 무수한 물방울을 만들어도
사랑하는 어머니 微動도 않으신다
발 밑 잡초가 키를 덮고 아카시아 뿌리가
입 속에 뻗어도 어머니, 뜨거운
어머니 입김 내게로 불어 온다

창을 닫고 귀를 막아도 들리는 빗소리,
사랑하는 어머니 비에 젖으신다
사랑하는 어머니 물에 잠기신다

I Heard Life Calling Me

when it rains again

my beloved mother is getting wet
my beloved mother is sinking in water
she doesn't make the slightest movement
even when the water penetrates her skin and her body swells
she doesn't make the slightest movement
even when the rainwater seeps deep inside her eyes
and creeps into her ears, forming legions of droplets
even when the weeds beneath her feet grow over her head and
    the acacia roots
fan out inside her mouth   my mother,
her hot breath blows toward me

even when I close the window and plug my ears,
I still hear the sound of rain
my beloved mother is getting wet in the rain
my beloved mother is sinking in water

어머니 1

가건물 신축 공사장 한편에 쌓인 각목더미에서 자기
　상체보다 긴 장도리로 각목에 붙은 못을 빼는 여인은
　남성, 여성 구분으로서의 여인이다 시커멓게 탄 광대뼈와
　퍼질러 앉은 엉덩이는 언제 처녀였을까 싶으잖다 아직
　바랜 핏자국이 水菊꽃 더미로 피어 오르는 오월,
　나는 스무 해 전 고향 뒷산의 키 큰 소나무 너머, 구름
　너머로 차올라가는 그녀를 다시 본다 내가 그네를 높이
　차올려 그녀를 따라잡으려 하면 그녀는 벌써 풀밭 위에
　내려앉고 아직도 점심 시간이 멀어 힘겹게 힘겹게
　장도리로 못을 빼는 여인,

어머니,
촛불과 안개꽃 사이로 올라오는 온갖 하소연을 한쪽 귀로
　흘리시면서, 오늘도 화장지 행상에 지친 아들의 손발에,
　가슴에 깊이 박힌 못을 뽑으시는 어머니......

I Heard Life Calling Me

mother 1

at the construction site of a new makeshift building the woman
   pulling nails from a pile of lumber with a clawed crowbar
   longer than her upper body is woman only in that she is
   biologically different from man   her sun-darkened
   cheekbones and the way she's sitting, buttocks splayed wide
   upon the ground, make me wonder just how long ago it was
   she'd been unmarried, young, virginal in May, the hydrangea
   blossoms a faded bloodstain hue, I see her as she was twenty
   years ago, vaulting up over the tall pine trees and over the
   clouds above the hill behind our house in our hometown
   I kick out to propel my swing to catch up with hers but she's
   already back down on the grass lunchtime's still far off, so she
   continues painstakingly, painstakingly to pull out nails,

oh mother,
while lamentations rising from the candles and baby's breath
   flowers stream past her ears, she pulls out the nails lodged
   deep within the hands and feet and chest of her son, again
   today exhausted from selling toilet paper on the street
   mother . . .

어머니 2

아직도 뜨거운 땡볕 아래 흰 수건으로 머리 동이시고
  펭귄처럼 가파른 계단을 뒤뚱거리며 오르시는 어머니,
  짐 진 하루 해가 공사판 건너 숲 속으로 지기가 그리
  힘들던가요 베니아판 흙 떨고 모로 누워도 熱덩어리 해는
  지지 않고 어머니, 당신이 잠깐 눈붙인 사이 동네방네
  애국 소리 딸꾹질 같아, 공사판 근처 일거리 없는 새들이
  가랑잎처럼 흩어집니다 어머니, 해고되고 해고되고
  떠돌아 목젖까지 차오르는 아우들이 바람 불지 않는
  가로를 날아갑니다 아직도 저들은 공사판 근처를
  기웃거리며 아내와 자식들 눈을 속인다고요

날아가세요, 어머니
날아가세요, 베니아판 집어 타고
해 떨어지는 곳으로!

mother 2

under the still scorching sun the mother toils up the steep stairs,
   swaying, penguin-like, a white cloth tied around her head
   is it so difficult for the sun, also lugging a load on its back,
   to traverse the construction site and set in the forest
   even after you brush the dirt from the plywood and stretch out
   on your side, that fiery fevered ball won't set   mother, while
   you catnap, the love-our-country clamor erupts like hiccups
   throughout the neighborhood, and around the construction
   site the birds without jobs scatter like dead leaves
   mother, the younger brothers, laid off again and again,
   have wandered much   anger has surged to their throats
   they fly over the windless streets   they're still hanging around
   construction sites, pretending, for their wives and children

fly away, mother
fly away, mount a slab of plywood, ride it
to where the sun sets!

수 박

여름날 오후 뜨거운 언덕받이를 타고 아파트로 가는 길엔
  어른이나 아이나 제 머리통보다 큰 수박 하나씩 비닐끈에
  묶어 들고 땀 흘리며, 땀 닦으며 정신없이 기어 오른다
  그들이 오르막 길에서 허우적거릴 땐 손에 달린 수박이
  떼구르르 구를 것도 같고, 굴러 내려 쇠뭉치로 만든
  공처럼 땅 속 깊이 묻혀 버릴 것도 같지만 무사히, 무사히
  수박은 개구멍 같은 아파트 현관 속으로 들어간다
그럼 이제 어떤 일이 벌어지는가 우선 끈에 묶인 수박을
  풀고 간단히 씻은 다음, 검은 등에 흰 배의 고등어 같은
  부엌칼로 떵떵 부은 수박의 배를 가르면, 끈적거리는 단
  물을 흘리며 벌겋게 익은 속이 쩍, 갈라 떨어지고 쥐똥
  같은 검은 알이 튀어 나온다 그러면 저마다 스텐
  숟가락을 손에 쥔 아버지와 할머니, 큰아이와 작은놈,
  머리를 뒤로 묶은 딸아이가 달겨들어 파먹기 시작하고,
  언제나 뒷처리하는 어머니는 이따금 숟가락 집어
  거들기도 하지만, 어머니는 입맛이 없다
어느새 수박씨는 마루 여기저기 흩어지고 허연 뱃대기를
  드러낸 수박 껍데기가 깨진 사기 접시처럼 쌓일 때,
  아이들은 자리를 박차고 뛰쳐 나가고 할머니는 건넌방에
  드러눕고 아버지는 값싼 담배를 붙여 물고, 게으르고 긴
  연기를 뿜을 것이다

watermelon

one summer afternoon on the hillside path up to the apartment block
    families, children as well as adults toil upward, sweating, wiping
    away the sweat, each lugging a plastic twine-netted watermelon larger
    than their heads   as they grab at the air for balance it seems that the
    melons dangling from their hands will go rolling down the hill and
    like balls of iron bury themselves at the bottom   but the melons make
    their way safely, safely into the cubbyhole entrance of the building
now what happens   the members of a family first undo the
    twine   they wash the melon and with a kitchen knife
    resembling a black-backed, white-bellied mackerel they split
    open the swollen-to-bursting stomach   sweet sticky juice
    seeps from the ripe red insides, and black seeds like rat
    droppings pop out   then the father, the grandmother, the first
    son, the second son, the pony-tailed daughter, each wielding a
    stainless steel spoon fall upon the melon and dig into it
    the mother, who always finishes off whatever scraps remain,
    from time to time lifts her spoon and joins them, but without
    much appetite
finally, seeds strewn all about and pieces of naked white belly-rind
    stacked up like porcelain dishes, the children dash outside
    the grandmother lies down in her room   the father lights
    a cheap cigarette and blows out long lazy streams of smoke

(continued)

수 박

그것은 어느 여름 어른들이 겪었다던 물난리 같은 것일까
질퍽하고 구질구질한 난장판 같은 것일까 아버지의
작업복을 기워 만든 걸레로 마루바닥을 훔치며 어머니는
바닥 여기저기 묻어 있는 수박물을 볼 것이다 벌건,
그러나 약간은 어둡고, 끈끈한 수박물을...... 왠지
쓸쓸해지기만 하는 어떤 삶을...

watermelon

is this similar to that calamitous flood the older people tell us they lived
through one summer   is it similar to that turbid squalid mess
wiping the floor with a rag she'd made from the father's old work clothes
the mother comes upon watermelon juice that's dribbled down here and
there upon the floor, watermelon juice, red, dark red, sticky . . . a life of
deepening loneliness . . .

聖母聖月 1

그날 꽃들은 부끄러운 가슴과 눈물겨운 뿌리를 쓰다듬으며
피어 오르고 봄은 달아나는 애인처럼 꽃 속에 묻혀 자꾸
죽고 싶어했다 봄은 아랫도리를 가리지 않은 아이처럼
길가에서 방뇨했고 후후, 뜨거운 입김을 뿜으며 음료수
가게로 달려갔다 아름다운 오월 건조한 고기압의 땅에서
우리는 자꾸 죽고 싶었다. 그날 사마리아 여인들과 함께
미사를 볼 때 버드나무 꽃가루가 창을 넘어 들어왔고
우리는 자꾸 죽고 싶었다, 죽을 생각은 없이 천주의
어린 양, 세상의 죄를 없애시는 주여......늙은 양들의
기도는 간절했고 우리는 자꾸 죽고 싶었다 흰 나룻배보다
긴 꽃잎 속에 몸을 감고, 눈부시고 목메어 고개 흔들며
무도 밟지 않은 땅을 가고 싶었다 아름다운 오월
버드나무 꽃가루가 눈을 덮을 때 미사는 끝났고 붉은
제단에서 식은땀이 흘렀다

holy mother, holy moon 1

that day, stroking their shy breasts and tearful roots, flowers
   burst upward into bloom and spring, like a lover who teases
   by running away, kept longing to die among the flowers
   like a bare-bottomed child spring peed on the street whew,
   whew, puffing hot breath from its mouth spring ran to a
   soda fountain on that lovely dry day in May, the country in
   the grip of a high pressure system, we kept longing to die
   that day, among the Samaritan women during Mass,
   willow-tree pollen wafting in through the windows, we
   kept longing to die, though not really wanting to God's little
   lamb, oh Lord who redeems the sins of the world . . . the
   prayers of the old sheep were sincere, and we kept longing to
   die, with our bodies wrapped inside flower petals longer
   than white wooden rowboats with our eyes blinded by
   brightness with our throats thick and our heads turning
   from side to side we wanted to get away to an unspoiled land
   the Mass on that lovely day in May ended when willow pollen
   blanketed our eyes and the red altar shed cold sweat

(continued)

聖母聖月 1

사랑의 어머니,
당신의 이름을 힘겹게 부를 때마다
임종의 괴로움을 홀로 누리시는 어머니,

불러주소서
그 눈짓, 그 음성으로
죄의 한 아이를......

holy mother, holy moon 1

oh, mother of love
each time I squeeze out your name
you suffer, all alone, the anguish of dying

please summon
with your voice and your eyes
a child who has sinned . . .

금빛 거미 앞에서

오늘은 노는 날이에요, 어머니
오랫동안 저는 잠자지 못했어요
오랫동안 먹지 못했어요 울지 못했어요
어머니, 저희는 금빛 거미가 쳐 놓은
그물에 갇힌 지 오래 됐어요
무서워요, 어머니
금빛 거미가 저희를 향해 다가와요
어머니, 무서워요
금빛 거미가 저희를 먹고
흰 실을 뽑을 거예요

in front of the golden spider

today's a day off, Mother
for a long time I haven't been able to sleep
for a long time I haven't been able to eat   I haven't been able to
    weep
Mother, for a long time
we've been trapped in the web of the golden spider
I'm scared, Mother
the golden spider's coming toward us
Mother, I'm scared
the golden spider will eat us
and spin out white thread

너의 깊은 물, 나를 가둔 물

괴로와하기 전에 기다리고
기다리기 어려울 때
한 번 숨을 끊고 들여다보는 물
너의 깊은 물, 나를 가둔 물

머리 풀듯이 괴로움 풀고
속절없이 한 세상 지나가면
이 물은 다시 흐를 것인가

형벌이여,
민물에 떠밀리는 이끼처럼
지금의 咽喉에 남아 있는
최초의 떨림!

your deep water, the water that dams me in

I wait before suffering pain
and when the waiting is difficult
I hold my breath and look within the water
your deep water, the water that dams me in

if like one untying her hair I release the pain
and unresisting let time go by
will the water flow again

what punishment
like moss swept along in fresh water,
all that remains in my throat now—
the initial stirring!

그대 위의 푸른 나뭇가지들

그대 위의 푸른 나뭇가지들
그 위로 밤,
그 위로 하늘, 갈라터진 별들

마음의 갈기가 잔잔히 흔들리고
잊혀진 곳에서 水門 열리는 소리

그대가 헤매는 거리를 다 헤매고
마침내 그대 자신을 헤맬 때
기다리라, 기다리라

奇跡적처럼 떠오를 푸른 잎사귀

green branches above you

green branches above you
night above the branches,
sky above the night, stars split open

my heart's mane flows tranquilly
and in a forgotten place the sound of a sluice gate opening

after you finish wandering in the place where you're wandering
and are at last wandering within yourself
you should wait, you should wait

for the green leaves that will, like a miracle, emerge

밤은 넓고 드높아

밤은 넓고 드높아 수없이 깔린 별들
서로 싸운다 더는 싸울 수 없는 순간에
별들은 낮게 내린다 더는 내릴 수 없는
순간에 별들은 내 몸에 달라붙는다

이것은 돌아가는 길인가, 오는 길인가
더는 다가설 수 없는 순간에 너를 부른다
네 얼굴을 보여다오,
바늘을 입에 문 물고기처럼

the night is high and wide

the night is high and wide and there are countless stars
they fight each other   when they can't fight more
they drop low   when they can't drop lower
they stick to my body

is this the road that takes me to where I'm going
or back to where I came from   when I can't get closer to you
I call out to you   please show me your face
a fish's, reeled in after taking the hook

요단을 건너는 저 가을빛

요단을 건너는 저 가을빛
물결을 지우며 달리는 나룻배 한 척
마음도 그와 같아서......

꺼지리라, 꺼지리라
저 불꽃 꺼지고 나면
거짓말로 위로하고 위로받으리라

crossing the Jordan, that autumnal color

crossing the Jordan, that autumnal color
a wooden rowboat flattens the waves
my heart is like that boat . . .

that flame will be extinguished, it will be extinguished
and after it is extinguished
I'll console someone, and by lying be consoled

이윽고 머릿 속에

이윽고 머릿속에 푸른 바람이 불고 잔모래가 날릴 때까지
　　그는 걸었다 마을과 숲과 바다를 지나 그가 서 있는 곳을
　　그는 확인할 수 없었다 어쩌면 家族들이 살고 있는 집
　　근처인지도 몰랐다 아무래도 좋았다

거기 얼마나 서 있어야 할지 몰랐다
애가 끓었다,
난로 위의 물주전자처럼

finally in his head

he walked on until finally in his head a blue wind blew and fine
   sand scattered   past a village   through a forest   by the ocean
   he wasn't sure where it was he was standing   possibly near
   the house his family lived in   but it didn't matter to him

he wasn't sure how much longer he'd stand there
he was agitated,
like water boiling upon a stove

어제는 하루종일 걸었다

어제는 하루종일 걸었다 해가 땅에 꺼지도록
아무 말도 할말이 없었다
길에서 창녀들이 가로막았다

어쩌면 일이 생각하는 만큼 잘못되지 않은 거라고
생각도 했다 어차피 마찬가지였다
가슴은 여러 개로 分家하여 떼지어 날아갔다

그것들이야 먼 데 계시는
내 어머니에게로 날아갈 테지만

젖은 불빛이 뺨에 흘렀다
날아가고 싶었다, 다만, 까닭을 알 수 없이

I walked all day yesterday

I walked all day yesterday until the sun sank beneath the ground
I had nothing to say
on the streets prostitutes blocked my way

it occurred to me that maybe things had not gone as wrong
as I'd thought   but even so it made no difference
my heart broke into many families that flew off in flocks

I knew they'd fly
to my mother who was far away

moist light streamed down my cheeks
I too wanted to fly away, though not knowing why

그의 집 지붕 위엔

그의 집 지붕 위엔 두 개의 尖塔이 솟아 있었다
아버지, 하고 그는 큰 소리로 불렀다

폐가 앞에서 삼 년을 기다리다가
그는 또 걷기 시작했다 자기를 무너뜨리며

온종일 그는 걸었다 자기를 무너뜨리며
다시 걸었다 어두운 궁릉에선 胎兒처럼 꼬부리고 잤다
일어나 다시 걸었다

좋은 약도, 사랑도 소용 없이
그는 걸어갔다 熱덩어리 해가 꺼지지 않는 길을

the roof of his house

two spires rose from the roof of his house
Dad, he called loudly

having waited three years in front of the desolate house
he resumed his walk, undoing himself

all day he walked, undoing himself
he walked again   curled fetus-like he slept inside a lightless
    dome
rousing himself he walked again

medicaments did not help, nor did love
he walked the road where the fireball sun is never extinguished

고통 다음에 오는 것들

고통 다음에 오는 것들,
저 하늘엔 밀고 밀리는 배들,
정다운 사람들은 명절날처럼 盛裝하고
떡과 과일을 나누고
나뉘는 슬픔의 몫도 아름답다

고통 다음에 돌아와
저무는 들판을 양팔로 껴안고
저미는 벌레 소리에 머리 수그리면

마침내 괴로움이 켜드는 불,
저 하늘엔 밀고 밀리는 배들,
착한 어버이들이 모여앉아
맑은 술을 나누고 있다

what comes after pain

what comes after pain,
boats in the sky nudging and being nudged,
friendly people dressed as for a holiday
sharing sweet-rice cakes and fruit
and, beautifully, their sadness

after pain I come back
with both arms embrace the field at sunset
bow my head to the poignant sounds of insects

and finally the flame that pain ignites,
boats in the sky nudging and being nudged,
kindhearted parents sitting together
sharing pure fresh wine

오래 고통받는 사람은

오래 고통받는 사람은 알 것이다
지는 해의 힘 없는 햇빛 한 가닥에도
날카로운 풀잎이 땅에 처지는 것을

그 살에 묻히는 소리 없는 괴로움을
제 입술로 핥아 주는 가녀린 풀잎

오래 고통받는 사람은 알 것이다
그토록 피해 다녔던 치욕이 빽빽한,
빽빽한 사랑이었음을

소리 없이 돌아온 부끄러운 이들의 손을 잡고
맞대인 이마에서 이는 따스한 불,

오래 고통받는 이여
네 가슴의 얼마간을
나는 덥힐 수 있으리라

those who have suffered long

those who have suffered long will understand
the sharp-edged blades of grass bending low to the ground
with the soft rays of the setting sun

the fine grass licks with its lips
the silent pain deep in its flesh

those who have suffered long will understand
that the shame they have been fleeing from is,
after all, just a stiff unyielding love

as those who have suffered long hold hands with those who,
    chagrined, have quietly returned
from their conjoined foreheads a warming fire starts,

you who have suffered long,
I can possibly bring warmth to
a part of your heart

높은 나무 흰꽃들의 燈

근심으로 가는 짧은 길에 노란 꽃들이 푸른 회초리 같은
  가지 위에 떨고, 높은 나무 흰꽃들이 燈을 세운다
  어디로 가도 무서운 길의 어느 입구에도 흰꽃들의
  燈이 자꾸 떨어지고, 갈수록 어둠 한쪽 켠은 환하고
  편하고, 병풍처럼 열리는 숲의 한가운데서 오래 전 새
  소리 자지러진다

——용서받지 못했던 날의 잘못이
이마의 못처럼 아프다

아이들아,
우리 살던 날들의 웃음을
다시 웃는 너희 얼굴에
수줍은 우리, 그림자 진다

white flower lanterns on tall trees

on the short path to worry yellow flowers tremble from
    branches that are like green whips, and on the tall trees white
    flowers are lantern-bright as I move along, at every opening
    off this dark and fearsome path white flower lanterns are
    falling   the deeper in I go the brighter and more comforting a
    corner of the darkness grows   in the middle of the forest,
    which opens like a folding screen, shrill sounds from birds of
    long ago

—the wrongdoing I did in my time, that can't be forgiven,
hurts like a nail in my forehead

children,
your faces smiling the smile
that we in our time smiled
make us shy, shadows fall upon us

초록 가지들은 燐光의 불을 켜 들고

비가 온다 오늘 저녁에도 나무는 그의 불안을 둥글고
    화목한 집으로 만든다 젖어 초록 가지들은 燐光의 불을
    켜 들고 불과 불 사이, 어두운 데를 골라 부리 긴 새들은
    불편한 잠을 준비한다

어디엔들 못 가랴,
바람에 몸 비비는 權木들 앞세우고
私有地의 무너지고 머리 드는
거친 숨결의 밤을 지나

어느덧 우리 둥근 나무의 품 속에서
부리 긴 새들의 불안한 꿈이 될 때까지

green branches emit a phosphorescent glow

it rains   again this evening the tree makes of its discomfort a round
   and peaceful home   its wet green branches emit a phosphorescent
   glow and the birds with the long beaks seek out dark places among
   the branches and prepare for their uneasy sleep

where can't we go,
staying ahead of us the bushes rub their bodies against the wind
we move through private land, the night breathing heavily,
drooping then raising its head

until eventually we become the uneasy dream
of the birds with the long beaks in the round nest of the tree

새벽 세시의 나무

빛이 닿지 않는 깊은 품 속에서 새벽 세시의 나무는 죽음을
  만든다 보이지 않는 공간에서 보이는 공간으로 그의
  죽음이 푸른 가지를 뻗고 나무는 가장자리의 잎들을
  흔든다 의지와 자세를 잊고 새벽 세시의 나무는 서 있다

언제나 초록의 싱싱함을 만드는 죽음은
빛이 닿지 않는 깊은 품 속에서
부리 긴 새의 잠을 흔든다

the tree at three in the morning

the tree at three in the morning begets death deep within its bosom
     where light can't reach   death lengthens the green branches, from
     unseen to seen, and the tree rattles the leaves of its outer branches
     the tree at three in the morning, lacking will or disposition, stands
                                                    oblivious

death, continuously creating green freshness
deep within the bosom of the tree where light can't reach,
rattles the sleep of the birds with the long beaks

남해 금산

한 여자 돌 속에 묻혀 있었네
그 여자 사랑에 나도 돌 속에 들어갔네
어느 여름 비 많이 오고
그 여자 울면서 돌 속에서 떠나갔네
떠나가는 그 여자 해와 달이 끌어주었네
남해 금산 푸른 하늘가에 나 혼자 있네
남해 금산 푸른 바닷물 속에 나 혼자 잠기네

South Sea, Silk Mountain

a woman was immured in stone
for her love I followed her into the stone
one summer it rained a lot
weeping, she left the stone
led by sun and moon she left
I'm alone now at the edge of the blue sky
   above Silk Mountain by the South Sea
alone I sink into the blue water of the South Sea at Silk Mountain

Appendix I

Excerpt of translators' interview with Yi Sŏng-bok in Taegu, October 13, 2003.

Q. According to the critics, *When Does a Rolling Stone Awaken* was revolutionary, and it opened a new way for poetry in the 1980s. In your opinion, how were your poems different from those of other Korean poets? Was it your intention to make them different?

A. In the beginning, I didn't study Korean poetry. I started as a foreign literature major, and was strongly influenced by foreign literature. Most [Korean] poets begin writing with echoes in mind of Kim So-wŏl and Han Yong-un. The only Korean poet influential for me at the time was Kim Su-yŏng. Poets more influential at that early stage were Celan, Mandelstam, and Pavese. I borrowed a lot from foreign writers. For example, in regard to social and political situations, I adopted Kafka's model—the relationship between father and son, the idea of seeing the family structure as a microcosm of the society, and the idea of seeking realism through symbols. These ideas weren't too familiar to many Koreans at the time. My thinking was then based on Western-style pessimism. That pessimism . . . which is rooted in Western philosophy . . . is different from nihilism. It's the attitude of struggling, yet knowing you're going to lose. Since my narrative techniques originated in Western literature, and my major was French, I naturally used a lot of surrealism. Surrealism did exist in Korean literature at the time, but as no more than a meaningless and unintelligible literary technique. My surrealism was unique in that it was meaningful. It was closely linked to the social and political situation of Korea at the time. I also introduced the technique of combining words and ideas in such a way that they would strongly influence and shock. My use of that technique to portray Korean situations, and my developing the idea that the ordinary life of an individual could be conceived as a reflection of social and political situations was also new. What I was doing was probably what the Korean critics now call deconstruction. But compared to the deconstruction they discuss these days, which is more philosophical and ideological, my deconstruction was more practical and realistic.

Q. You just said that deconstruction before you was ideological, and that yours was practical. This is similar to what you said in your interview with the poet Yi Mun-je. Was that something you were thinking about at the time you were writing your poems, or something that occurred to you afterward?

A. Of course my interpretation now is based on my current point of view. Deconstruction and post-structuralism were merely terms that critics later applied to the poems. The surrealistic techniques and Western-style imagination and tragic sensibility of my poetry weren't the results of logical or ideological thinking, but a natural consequence of my being alive and experiencing the real world at that time. They were physical manifestations of the time. The concept of deconstruction didn't exist at the time. It was adopted later, as the word was introduced in Korea. How was my poetry related to deconstruction? It violated, with its iconoclasm, existing poetic form and content. In this sense, deconstruction is no more than an after-the-fact term.

Q. Many critics say the poems in *When Does a Rolling Stone Awaken* are cynical and pessimistic. Do you agree? Do you think those two descriptive words fairly describe your poems?

A. Basically, cynicism and pessimism were the themes of my imagination. They still are. As I mentioned earlier, struggling while knowing you are going to lose is the main theme of my life and poetry. In life, one can sometimes have fun, and sometimes be forgetful. But in the present, as in the past, it is through my poetry that I live my life, which is doomed to be a losing game. If I deal with social issues, my voice can be satirical. But whether I deal with social issues or explore my inner self, I always have the same motif—pessimistic imagination. It appeared in my first book of poetry, and again in my recent poetry. . . . I always see the pessimistic in life. Pessimism has to do with the pride of being human. Greek tragedies are about the failures of humans, yet at the same time about human dignity. The protagonists, kings and such, have noble stature. They don't try to compromise, or to forget about things, as we ordinary people do. They struggle until the end, until they fall. That's what I mean by human dignity— unyielding until the end.

Q. According to the critic Yi Sŭng-hun, there is in *When Does a Rolling Stone Awaken* a lot of black humor, which functions as a mask to conceal your depression and despair. Could you please talk about your use of black humor?

A. Humor in general provides comfort and joy for an audience. In contrast, black humor confronts it with the horror of life. Black humor reveals the underlying structure of our lives. Experienced from the outside, black humor is humorous. But from within, there is darkness and misery. The outside humor exaggerates and even increases the internal darkness and misery. My narrative techniques are sometimes the opposite of the techniques of black humor. One of my techniques is extreme realism. Another is romanticism, a yearning for the soft and delicate. This means that black humor isn't all I'm after. I'm also seeking what's precious and dear in life, those few things that remain beneath the ashes of a house that's burned to the ground. So I hope my readers discern the efforts I make to revive the traces of warmth that remain, the few embers that have not been completely extinguished. . . . Because my first book is seemingly violent and contentious, people tend to think that there is no such trace. But they'll still admit that what makes the contentiousness bearable is that coexistent with it is also a yearning for the maternal and the feminine. In that sense, I'm neither a Dadaist nor a pure surrealist.

Q. You've suggested that a yearning for the feminine, for softness, is also present in *When Does a Rolling Stone Awaken*. Can you cite a specific example? Are you talking about the sister and the mother who appear in a number of the poems?

A. My first book describes the world of the father, the second the world of the mother, though the mother does appear in the first book as well. It's true that in the first book the world of mother and sister is often crushed and corrupted by the violence of the paternal world. But this doesn't mean that mother and sister are violent or corrupted. They are always helplessly victimized. Violence can exist because of the existence of the delicate and the feminine. Violence occurs because there is always someone subjected to it, and that is the dynamic that sustains the structure of violence. I suspect that this aspect of my poetry is always overlooked. Any talk about hope in the structure of violence should be about the mother and the sister, who are not the practitioners of violence themselves but who suffer from it. It is violence and pretension, not the world of the victims—mother and sister—that is negated in my poems.

Q. Critics talk about how your poems are continuously changing from book to book. What motivated you to change? What led you to move from society to individual, from external to internal?

A. There are two types of writers. One is the settling type, the sédentaire, the other the nomadic type. I'm a typical nomad—a brand-tiller. A brand-tiller doesn't stay in one place and can't stand staying in one place. If one problem is solved, he has to move on to another. If he has tried one way of solving a problem, he tries another. Why? Because life is short. While I'm alive, I'd like to visit the U.S., Turkey, Africa, etc. I'd like to exhaust all the possibilities of life. Andre Gide talked about two aspects of youth. [Yi here switched from Korean to English and French.] One is sincérité—the attitude of youth, not to deceive the self or the others. The other is disponibilité—the openness of mind to all possibility. It's the essence of his essay "Les Nourritures Terrestres." That's literature. Terrestre. The globe, the earth, the nurture of the earth. Disponibilité and sincérité. A motto of mine. [Here Yi returned to Korean.] This is why I try many different possibilities. I'm a typical nomad type. I don't know how much more I'll be writing before I die, but I'd like to try all different possibilities. If one ties a stone to one end of a string, and holding the other end whirls the string, the stone will arc a circle in the air while the center of the circle remains fixed in the hand of the person. Likewise, my center remains in the same place although I'm drawing circles around the center.

Q. Weren't there also external causes contributing to the shift of tone and focus?

A. One reason for the shift of tone and focus is that when I was writing my first book, society was in political chaos. It was dominated by irrationalities. That was the number one problem threatening our existence. People were being victimized and arrested. When I was writing the poems in the second book, the social situation had improved. Another reason is that as I got older, I became more interested in human existence than in social issues. There are poets of my generation who are still interested in social problems. . . . I'm not saying that social issues are of less importance. I'm simply more concerned about fundamental human issues. . . . To me, violence still matters.

Q. In the poem "Christmas," you express a great deal of sympathy for Pavese. You seem to identify with him, you become the room he was in when he killed himself. Were you thinking of suicide when you wrote the poem?

A. I'm so afraid, and cowardly. I love life in spite of all the ugliness, of all the monstrous things about life. Recently I read a book by a German writer about Pavese and Nietzsche. They both lived in Torino. Pavese committed suicide in Torino. I recently read his plays. I love him very much. I love him more than any others. Can you understand? He was delicate and sensitive. And he had an unhappy love life. He killed himself because of a woman.

Appendix 2

A Training to Live without Happiness—
the Poetic World of Yi Sŏng-bok*

Hwang Tong-kyu

1

These days, when I'm reading or writing poetry, the thought often occurs to me that the writing of poetry is a training to live without happiness. But that's not completely true. Poetry should be able to sing also of happiness, and to show us individuals who have broken free from the magnetic field of our unhappiness-indulging Korean literature. Thinking further on it, I wonder if poets aren't after all rightly probing into unhappiness, if perhaps the human condition is such that people are unhappy because they are human.

What really matters is the poet's stand in resisting the pull to settle down in that magnetic field, not just because resistance builds individual character, and that makes for freshness, but because the spirit of resistance is the very beginning of art.

*This commentary appeared in the first edition of *When Does a Rolling Stone Awaken.*

Having developed such an attitude of resistance, a poet will become aware of his role, however small, in reshaping the complex structure of the magnetic field into something more amenable to humanity. In this way, he will make art more meaningful to humans. However, the developing of such an attitude sometimes finds expression in singular poems, poems which can frustrate readers.

2

I imagine that many people have been frustrated reading Yi Sŏng-bok's poetry since it is completely unlike the poetry we've become accustomed to in recent years. On the surface his poetry appears similar to Kim Su-yŏng's but he is less analytical than Kim, making use instead of free associations and of the quality of consciousness that results. His free associations are linked together psychologically. This can be demonstrated in any poem selected at random. Let us first try the middle part of "exodus."

> even before I start off, the road, treading on itself,
> vanishes   it lies flat like dried squid
> I turn back and drink
> my girlfriend gets drunk first and sprawls on the ground
>
> I'm afraid that having stayed awake all night
> in the murk of the underpass I'll kill the Three Wise Men
> when they come talking nonsense

The road, which does not behave like a road, is compared to "dried squid." Dried squid naturally reminds us of drinking something alcoholic, which leads to his girlfriend's getting drunk. She sprawls on the ground. Sprawling on the ground, suggestive of being down, links to the image of being down in the underpass, and then to the memory of having stayed awake all night in the murk of the underpass. The words "awake" and "murk" add to the poetic effect. Having stayed awake all night signifies "waiting," which disposes readers to accept without resistance the Three Wise Men. "Nonsense" softens the harshness of "I'm afraid . . . I'll kill." Characters and objects, seemingly presented in random disorder, are in fact coherently arranged in terms of psychological cause and effect.

Now let's look at the beginning of "oral tale," which seems even more complicated.

> I'd like to eat cherries and give birth to an outrageous child
> to become a walking poem   a duck
> standing upside down   a vomiting toe
> a potato with toenails   a friendly
> factory . . .

The images—outrageous child, poem, duck, toe, potato, factory—follow one another, each tagged with a suitable modifier. The images are quite different from those used by some of the Korean surrealist poets, who simply indulge in showing things in an unusual arrangement—an operating table next to an umbrella, for example. Yi's images reveal the latent relationships between and among things that are closely linked.

Cherries are a fruit that is appetizing to pregnant women. Though apricots are better known for having this quality, I think Yi chose cherries because of their small and beautiful shape, which corresponds to the image of dew in the second stanza:

> I   the morning dew   a sparrow suspended in Mr. Yi's sunset

An "outrageous child" is a central motif of the poem. The adjective "outrageous" seems to fit naturally here with the narrator, a male, giving birth to a child.

The child that is born will grow and start walking. A "walking poem," therefore, is an image closely related to what precedes it.

Notable here is that "poem" and "outrageous child" are an identical pair.

Walking is linked to "standing upside down." Next, "a poem" is identified with "a duck." The image is an allusion to the Korean proverb "turning in duck's feet after eating someone else's chicken." A "duck's feet" poem makes us feel like vomiting. Vomiting reminds us of the nasty odor of toes, as well as of life that is like a potato. This leads to the image of a life with toenails. Then, thinking of a factory, which really is something ugly and unpleasant, we wish it would become something pleasant.

That is the chain reaction that began with cherries. But since the image of cherries is not any more important to the poem than the many other images, we can easily conceive of Yi's having bypassed a string of linked images that might have preceded cherries. Not starting a poem at its absolute beginning is a technique Yi used in other poems. The effect is that readers feel a sense of speed from the very first line. It's as though Yi skips the ignition scene and starts with the car already in motion and picking up speed. A sense of speed is one of the characteristic qualities of his poems. Any of his poems can serve as an example. Let's try "that day."

> that day my father left for Kŭmch'on on the seven o'clock
>> train
> and my younger sister went to school at nine   that day my
> mother's worn-out legs swelled like balloons and I went to the
> newspaper company and lazed around all day   the border
> with the North was secure and all was perfect in the world
> nothing was missing   that day prostitutes hung around the
> train station from mid-afternoon and girls who in a few years
> would become prostitutes helped at home with the house-
>> work
> or took care of their kid-brothers and sisters   that day my
> father had an argument with the president of his company
>> about collecting a debt for him and my younger sister

went to a concert with her boyfriend that day on my
way home I saw a trim woman in boots and thought you
can even kill someone you love that day not everything
that flew above the indifferent trees was a bird I saw
women weeding grass, weeding their own lives, and men
tearing down houses, tearing down their own sky I saw
an old fortune-teller with his fortune-telling bird and the
venerable jug he carried for when he had to pee that day
some people were killed in traffic accidents and down-
town that day the bars and love hotels were crowded as
usual but nobody heard that day's moaning all were
sick but nobody felt the pain

There probably aren't many poems equal to this in the rapid-
ity of description. The first-person narrator not only observes the
situation of the father, the mother, and the younger sister, he is
also actively involved. In this poem there is also a string of images:
the father's "leaving," the sister's "going," the mother's "legs"—the
physical organ that carries out leaving and going. Unlike the three
people associated with legs or leg movement, the narrator "lazed
around all day" at the newspaper company. "Lazing around" links
to "secure," and "secure" to "perfect." If the world is perfect, noth-
ing is lacking, not even prostitutes. In this manner the poem leads
us in the end to the "moaning" and to those who are sick but do
not feel the pain.

Are these images clichés? Far from it. We feel that the many
images in the three poems cited are daring. Yi's poems consist
of daring images and thoughts linked naturally together. Where,
then, do we find the essence of Yi's poems?

3

It's risky to attach labels to artists. But we sometimes take that risk
for the sake of convenience. If we had not had lots of experience

in the past with dilettante poets who called themselves "surrealists," we probably would have readily labeled Yi Sŏng-bok a surrealist. Surrealists were most interested in strings of images. They wanted to liberate people through the release of the subconscious. The liberation would come about as a result of the weakening of the ego—the basis of logical thinking—and the consequent freeing of the id, the subconscious, which is more fundamental. The subconscious produces irrational, but daring and primal images. Our dilettante poets, interested in the collision of such images—a subsidiary surrealistic technique—simply copied the technique. There is no evidence that they paid attention to the essence of surrealism, which is both the destruction of the ego and of the petit bourgeois lifestyle in which the ego resides, and the human pain and joy in the carrying out the destruction. For that reason, most of what was written by those earlier Korean surrealists appears to be clumsy wordplay.

Iconoclasm inevitably accompanies the destruction of the petit-bourgeois lifestyle. It is not accidental that the symbolically iconoclastic destruction of the father is a characteristic of Yi's poems. This is not to say that iconoclasm automatically becomes surrealism. Iconoclasm should occur simultaneously with irrationalism, the liberation of the subconscious. There are poets such as Oh Kyu-won who are also iconoclastic in their poems but we don't call them surrealists, because their destructions are the product of common sense and rationality. Anyway, one needs to be cautious in labeling poets. It is essential not to use labels in making judgments about poets.

Iconoclastic irrationality occurs throughout Yi's poems.

Eli, Eli please do not die   be nailed instead to my naked
    parched body
though you have only one body, you're able to die as often as
    you choose   a death of substance   please show me the
flowers you raised   Eli, Eli when you ascend to heaven

I'll cross over into death, and that's it   the spoiled body
of your daughter—your mother—will be married off, even after
     she dies   ["in a congenial brothel"]

the displacement of the men of the plant and grass-eating
     tribe
not bothering the children playing in the empty lots
and locking up the women inside the dressmakers' shops,
the hairdressers' shops, the kitchens, the Mongol troops
called us out by numbers   number 53, into the guts of a
chicken   number 54, into a condom   number 55, onto the
point of a sword   go, right now   this land was bought as an
investment by a corporate tycoon yesterday   where you
planted your right foot is owned by a movie star   where
you peed belongs to a sister of a boxer's mistress   where
the cricket chirped all night is the property of a member of
the Art Academy   ["displacement"]

the postman doesn't take the letter   at times he does take it
while having a drink he opens it and reads it aloud . . .
my dearest,   damn it   today I finally will write a letter
                             ["a letter"]

Once we start looking for examples of iconoclasm, we'll find
them throughout the book. In Yi's poems, everything—love, fam-
ily, country, adult life, etc.—is satirized, destroyed, and dissolved.

The destruction, however, does not occur violently or too ex-
plicitly, partly because of his natural stringing together of images
and his narrative speed, primarily because he created artistic dis-
tance between reality and his poetry. His poetry has the quality of
a black-and-white film. His poems, full of strings of images and
fantasies, do not present fantastic colors; they tend to be mono-
chromatic. This holds true whether he is depicting leaves, women,
fathers. Only black and white stand out.

at the base of the mountain, blocking out the white hospital
building a train was stalled. (some cars were loaded with coal
others were just dark mouths full of water)

[“in front of the house of years”]

The contrast between black and white is stark. Yi's use of col-
ors other than black and white is extremely limited. There are
times that different colors appear, as in the following poem.

Pyŏkjae. a place where the restaurant, grocery store, bicycle
shop signs are dilapidated, where the *mu* flowers grow yellow
in small vegetable gardens and the sound of dogs howling is
heard along the road where plastic bags blow about.
Pyŏkjae. you should not go there if it's difficult for you to say
good-bye. Pyŏkjae. a broken bridge.

[“Pyŏkjae”]

The color yellow here is not realistic. *Mu* flowers are not yel-
low, but close to purple or white. The narrator might insist that
his *mu* flower is a variety but I don't think that makes sense, con-
sidering the context of the poem. The factory, the bicycle shop,
and the plastic bags are characteristically black and white.

Sometimes the “white” in his poems even has the tonal grada-
tions of monochromatic films.
that winter the snow piled high as my thigh
when I opened the window the mountain, snow-masked,
soared upward, saying “aah”

[“snow”]

The tonality of black-and-white films in his poems sets him
apart from Andre Breton and other French symbolists, who made
use of fantastic colors. This shows that Yi was both an idiosyn-
cratic surrealist, and a surrealist in a narrower sense. This also gives

I Heard Life Calling Me

us an indication of the emotional pain he must have sustained as a result of being unique and special.

4

From "1959," the first poem in the book, to "now only about love that came at the wrong time, too late," the last poem, there are intimations of a hurt, or a wounding, which we cannot put a specific name to.

> that year, though winter ended and summer began
> spring did not come   the peach tree
> bore tiny fruits before flowering
> and the barren apricot withered
>
> ["1959"]

> the calf of your leg is sliced by an unseen sword
>
> ["spring night"]

> when you think back, there are words that become blood
> words that seek out and settle in your wounds and brandings
>
> ["you don't know what you're shaking"]

> now about a thigh pierced by an awl rather than about the
>   awl
> about caked-dry eyelids and disfigured lips
>
> ["now only about love that came
>   at the wrong time, too late"]

In almost all his poems there are examples of pain associated with the hurt/wound. The pain is not a record of the carnal victory such as entailed in the primal sin of the West. It is rather an integral part of the human condition, with which Yi is obsessed. This theory can be confirmed by the fact that a sensual poem like "in the realm of water" ends with crying and an "anguished mouth."

> if you're the water's feet I'm its toes
> if you're the water's bell I'm its sound
> worming and muscling
> in among the molecules, rubbing up against their flesh
> if you're the water's mouth, the parted mouth of water,
> I'm the tears that link heaven to earth   oh, if you're the
>   anguished mouth of water

The hurt/wound is not something that can be easily healed, or understood, through a sociological approach. It is of the kind described in "the river never returns."

> I fell asleep in a field of grass   my body cracked like the shell
>   of a water bird's egg and a wingless dream crawled out

And in "for Lara," one of the rare poems about happiness in the book, the final line is "you peck at the asphalt road with a happy beak and squash your shit with happy feet."

In a way, the pain might be for Yi a condition of living in Korea, a condition possibly related intimately to something psychological that is difficult for him to express in rational terms. In any case, it is also true that, by airing that condition, he enjoys a kind of freedom, or a sense of liberation.

Thinking of such condition, in which love, happiness, the wind are all blighted, let me return to the beginning of this commentary—to the idea of a training to live without happiness, to a life of singing about a lack of happiness, and to all those ideas that are possibly untrue. This book of poems does not depict people who are trying to get away from the magnetic field or from the conditions in which they are living. It rather depicts the psychological freedom of people who have managed to break away.

Maybe this has its origin in Yi's oppressed youth, or maybe in the nature of city life, subject as it is to the contamination and polluting effects of increasing industrialization. Or maybe it is the consciousness of our time. Whatever the reason, unless Yi manages to create fresh images of people who are unhappy because they are human, and of their struggles to break away from their living conditions, the narrow range of his subject matter and the limitations of his palette might lead to a melting away of his uniqueness. But then again, maybe it would be worthwhile for him to stick with his style to the end. We have heard his voice. Now we will probably just have to wait and see what direction he takes, whether he soars skyward, or disappears into the earth.

Appendix 3

Poetic Variations on the Theme of Shame*

Kim Hyŏn

Those who read Yi Sŏng-bok's poetry without paying close attention may become frustrated by the profound differences among his poems. Sometimes there is a description of a situation difficult to understand, like something from a fantasy novel, sometimes a sudden outcry, but without sufficient explanation for it. As a result, his poems can leave readers feeling depressed and empty, wondering if the time and effort they invested in trying to understand and enjoy his poems was wasted. That is the final obstacle to overcome. If readers would be patient, and read his poems slowly and repeatedly, they would discover in them a cohesiveness, which not only contributes to the coherence of each poem but also situates, to quote a Korean critic, Yi's "terrain." In the poems, readers can experience Yi's depression, hopes, and happiness, and encounter various remembered incidents from his past. Some poems are peaceful lyrics, others outcries of despair.

Yi's "terrain" is well-planned and controlled. It is of course the territory of the heart, a spiritual space within the poet's memory. In that space in memory, which he referred to as "the cat-

*This essay first appeared in the first edition of *South Sea, Silk Mountain.*

acombs"—an underground tomb—"there is no peace"; in that space are such images as "a mouth whose tongue fell out, a breast whose nipple fell off" [*from* "no peace in memory"]. Because there is no peace in his memories, his dreams tend to be nightmarish, as in the poem "amazing, how amazing it is, every night of the shining sun." He consciously assembles memories, creates a poem, destroys the poem, then re-creates it. His two long, separately published poems—"a valley journal" (1982) and "the promised land" (1983)—are excellent poems of refined composition that he later completely deconstructed, and then reconstructed into a number of new poems. This deconstruction-reconstruction process indicates his growing realization that a refined poetic form is unsuitable for nightmares. A poet is a poet, and should therefore write good poems. But he was aware that good poems were not the right form for nightmares, that good poems and "the heavy breathing and the body heat" [*from* "a stillness"] are incompatible. So he chops his poems into small pieces, and, how amazing, the pieces join together and create their own spiritual form.

Yi's poetic deconstruction-reconstruction process is, on the one hand, an act of digging out a spiritual path, which is like "a shadow on the road where rainwater has pooled" [*from* "what was far away falls like raindrops"], and on the other hand, a poetic act by which he tries to perceive and understand the unity of the world through the recollections of his narrative self. He tries to re-create the universal patterns of life by fashioning poems from the nightmarish images trapped within the complicated maze of the underground tomb of memory, and then deconstructing and reconstructing the poems. The reason he keeps destroying and reassembling his memories is that "until you of a sudden notice me . . . I won't know where I'm going" [*from* "prelude"]. A person who does not know where he is going is someone who does not have a "sign" that can make him recognizable as himself. Can a person, who is like a shadow, be recognized as himself without his

I Heard Life Calling Me

"sign"? This question leads to a further question—why doesn't Yi have a sign? Why didn't he know where he was going? He does not describe in detail the nightmares of the "I," the narrator of his poems. Implied in the poems is that "something happened here, too shameful to talk about! shameful even for those who did not take part" [*from* "and again the fog descended"]. Because of whatever happened that could not be talked about, the people "spoke to each other in subdued voices." The implication is that the victim of the incident is the narrator's sister (or all sisters). "Only my sister knew what had happened," the narrator says. "I couldn't look at our dad, or trust him" [*from* "shame, like a tortoiseshell"]. What could possibly have happened between father and sister? Characteristic of Yi's poems is the prompting of such questions. But even more characteristic is that the questions spawn larger questions. He expands the meaning of the incident "too shameful to talk about" into something larger than a personal matter, so that it can be re-questioned from a general and public perspective. Something happened here. But no one talked about it. That is shameful, shameful because no one talked about it. "Even when like snow it [shame] melts, it immediately hardens again / shame leaks from the hollowed eyes of a man unable for days to sleep" [*from* "about shame"]. The shame is so strong that the narrator is unable to sleep for days. But the father doesn't say anything. That too is shameful. The father is not just the narrator's father, but all fathers, including the fathers of his father: "our ancestors were often crying they were crying beneath the roots of the grass my sister, what we believed to be sky turned out to be a field of loose gravel" [*from* "our ancestors were often crying"]. The ancestors too, are silent. That too is shameful. Why don't they talk?

oh shame
a bowl of rice
still steaming!

["an end to shame"]

Shame is caused by a bowl of rice. Or shame is rice itself. Looking at the world from the point of view of shame, "nothing that was promised has been done / the older women, after crying, have fallen asleep under the low eaves and the children, smelling of fish, are still playing in the deep water   the strong are still strong, and the weak are endlessly building a pyramid / swindle, theft, murder, swindle, theft, theft, murder . . ." [*from* "the promised land"]. In neighborhoods where the poor live, the flowers "bloomed like a rash" [*from* "the grass that grows at the bottom of river"], and in the river beside which children are playing, "fish, tangled in detergent bubbles, gasped for breath" [*from* "a child carrying a doll on her back"]. Life there is "like a landscape, hazy with blowing dust, that we see as through an old dusty window" [*from* "once again spring came"], and so "even without there being severe pain days passed and people suffered silently" [*from* "even without there being severe pain"]. These are places where "words are not understood . . ." where "you can't even depend upon a prophet   his stomach's full   he has no worries" [*from* "the forest of tall pine trees"]. The narrator profoundly distrusts prophets and righteous people.   However, the narrator is still alive. Remaining alive is life's ultimate desire. "There was a faint light that could not be extinguished   ah, how I wish it would be, I murmured   it wasn't" [*from* "the faint light could not be extinguished"]. Why, not having found a reason to live, is the narrator still alive? Not having a reason to live, he should end his life. He intends to do so by surrendering his body to the river of death—"pretty soon this hungering too will be cut off   fine dust will cover the rattling drawer of memory   moss, blood-stained by the water flowing in our noble mountains and rivers, will blanket the sounds of breathing   pretty soon, pretty soon, my itching tongue will grow moldy, and alien death will envelop my white blood cells" [*from* "pretty soon, this hungering too"]. However, someone intervenes—his mother takes upon herself his shame: "while lamentations rising from the candles and baby's breath flowers stream past her ears, she pulls out the nails lodged deep within the hands and feet and chest of her son, again today exhausted from selling toilet paper on the street . . ." [*from* "mother 1"]. The "mother" poems give us a mother figure symbolizing acceptance and tolerance, in contrast to the father figure's symbolizing reality and rules. These are outstanding poems. With sensitivity and restraint they portray the Korean mother, who leads "a life of deepening loneliness . . ." [*from* "watermelon"]. How many tears are concealed within that restraint! But the narrator severs his connection with his mother and returns to "the water that dams me in / if like one untying her hair I release the pain / and unresisting let time go by / will the water flow again" [*from* "your deep water, the water that dams me in"]. Is the passage to death "the road that takes me to where I'm going, or back to where I came from?" [*from* "the night is high and wide"]. Whether a "going to" or a "returning to," the passage to death is a journey of wandering. "All day he walked, undoing himself / he walked again   curled fetus-like he slept inside a lightless dome" [*from* "the roof of his house"]. The passage to death is a passage of rebirth. After all, the road going to is the same as the road coming from. Having wandered for a long time, the narrator realizes that "the shame they [those who have suffered long] have been fleeing from is, / after all, just a stiff unyielding love" [*from* "those who have suffered long"]. This realization leads the narrator to a sense of community; he feels he can now bring human warmth to those who suffer. The wisdom he acquired in the passage to death is succinctly expressed in images proposing that death is life and life is death:

> death, continuously creating green freshness
> deep within the bosom of the tree where light can't reach,
> rattles the sleep of the birds with the long beaks
>
> > ["the tree at three in the morning"]

Isn't one of the long-beaked birds the narrator himself, who goes forth and returns? In the passage to death, shame is wisely accepted, and the shamed sister is mythicized, becoming a symbol of the wisdom of acceptance. The narrator is now alone "at the edge of the blue sky above Silk Mountain by the South Sea . . ." Alone he "sink[s] into the blue water of the South Sea at Silk Mountain." In front of him we see the shamed woman, being led by the sun and the moon.

> a woman was immured in stone
> for her love I followed her into the stone
> one summer it rained a lot
> weeping, she left the stone
> led by sun and moon she left
> I'm alone now at the edge of the blue sky
>   above Silk Mountain by the South Sea
> alone I sink into the blue water of the South Sea at Silk
>   Mountain
>
> ["South Sea, Silk Mountain"]

Something happened here. The shamed sister, after being comforted by the narrator's love, leaves, weeping. She appears to be mythical in that she is led by sun and moon—in other words, by nature and time. In other words, this is a story of a universal truth.

In these poems, Yi's narrator is undergoing a mythical rite of passage, consisting of four stages: his shame-filled life, his mother's attempt to prevent him from dying, his journey into the world of death, his return. During the passage he meets with hardships, overcomes them, dies, and returns to life. The rite of passage is both internal and external. It is also a narrative passage, in that it shows both the beginning and the end. The lyrical self sees life and all it consists of, recollected as through a hazy moonlit nimbus. In this sense, the passage is not lyrical. It differs from the lyrical in that it proceeds through a linear development of incidents. This inevitably leads us to the question: does this mean that Yi has written a book of narrative, not lyrical poems?

Indeed, this book has many narrative characteristics. First of all, it has a narrative story line, which consists of the following nuclear units:

The narrator enters the catacomb of memory.
The narrator's sister has a humiliating experience.
The narrator wants to die.
The narrator's mother intervenes.
The narrator sets off on a journey toward death.
The narrator returns.

The last three units are very much narrative. The mother is "the woman pulling nails from a pile of lumber with a clawed crowbar longer than her upper body." In the poem "mother 1," her son is "selling toilet paper on the street"; in the poem "mother 2" he is a laborer who has been "laid off again and again." The mother's family consists of "the father, the grandmother, the first son, the second son, the pony-tailed daughter" [*from* "watermelon"]. It is a poor, foul-smelling family.

Second, the narrator is in closer touch with his narrative self than with his lyrical self. The following poem, objectively descriptive, is a fine example.

among the autumn trees spattered sparsely with leaves
a woman shed her bridal gown and fell sleep upon it

a prodigiously fat black deer
inspected her bottomless sleep

["Tess"]

There are also many poems with monologues, stream of consciousness passages, etc. Since the narrator is in close touch with his narrative self, many images in the poems have a rational rather than an emotional or sensory basis: "the reason we're sick is that / life loves us . . . if we feel sorry for life we have no choice / but to be tied to it" [*from* "oh, the folding of time"]; "I guess there are times when an old tree would also like to be young again" [*from* "once again, spring came"]; "blood grins on the lips of these righteous people" [*from* "the forest of tall pine trees"]; "friendly people . . . sharing . . . beautifully, their sadness" [*from* "what comes after pain"]. In his poetics, Yi called this kind of wisdom "aphoristic." According to him, "understanding the futility of life enables one to make aphoristic statements . . . for example, when life is expressed as a heavy burden—as in Job of the Old Testament, as in soul music, as in ancient folk songs." The wisdom, then, of simultaneously accepting and rejecting life is clear. Yi believes that living ritualistically is unavoidable. Though he rejects the ritualistic life, he endeavors to find wisdom in it. The wisdom he finds is aphoristic.

But despite the many narrative qualities of the poems, we cannot categorize this book as a collection of narrative poems. Though the book is "an expression of the life of the group through the life of an individual—a poet," the nostalgia, desire, and tension expressed in the poems belong to Yi, an individual poet. In other words, the poet's private feelings are echoed throughout. Wherever he may be, he always comes back to himself.

> after you finish wandering in the place where you're
>   wandering,
> and are at last wandering within yourself
> > ["the green branches above you"]

The green leaves, which are, in their material form, an expression of the meaning of life, will, like a miracle, emerge. Perceiving that you are lost within yourself even when you are among others is the instinctive and intuitive awareness of the narrative self. Again, we cannot regard his poetry as simply lyrical.

One of the core questions this book poses is whether the narrative self can perceive and recognize the universality of the world, and if so, whether the narrative self can or cannot express it. Most poets try to resolve this question by replacing the lyrical self with the narrative self. For that reason, their poems are no more than prose works in verse form. Unique about Yi is that he has not abandoned his lyrical self, but has tried to adapt his narrative self to it, so that in his poems the world becomes a place in which the fundamental desires causing class struggle can be addressed, rather than a place where class struggle is enacted. Yi himself is the world, the arena of those desires which make the world shameful. Immersing oneself deeply in the physical sensations of the poems is the easiest way to enjoy reading this outstanding book.

> you are a beast, a star, a stillness
> burning hot at my fingertips
>
> ["you are a beast, a star"]

On reading these lines, it is much more pleasurable to indulge in the physicality of the beast, the star, the fingertips, the burning stillness, than to go digging for metaphysical meanings. The otherness of "you," an abstraction when considered metaphysically, can take on a vivid reality when conceived physically. Although "you" simultaneously contains the body, which is beastlike, and the non-body, which is starlike, when I touch "you" with my fingertips, "you" become for me, as for the narrator, a hot, silent flame. A burning sensuality is the true nature of the other. If we continue to explore Yi's sensations, that which is "screaming, crying, gyrating, tearing at my wild hair . . ." is physically expressed as "the madly rocketing jets of water from the rubber hoses at a car wash" [*from* "once again, spring came"]; slipperiness is expressed as "the noodles in a dish of *chapch'ae*" [*from* "even without there being severe pain"]. In a way, the rubber hoses, and the noodles in a dish of *chapch'ae* can be taken as phallic symbols. In the poem "my heart, do you still remember," Yi uses the physical images of laughter, dandelion fluff, and inflation to express lightness. Laughter links with white dandelion fluff (evoking an image of white teeth) which links with inflation, and these images cluster around and give significance to the concept of lightness. The images work because of Yi's poetic talent in communicating physical sensations.

> he wasn't sure how much longer he'd stand there
> he was agitated,
> like water boiling upon a stove
>
> ["finally in his head"]

This poem is another clear example. But what impresses me more than his poetic talent with words are such lines as in the following poem, in which he describes tears shining in the light of a street lamp as "moist light."

> my heart broke into many families that flew off in flocks
>
> I knew they'd fly
> to my mother who was far away
>
> moist light streamed down my cheeks
> I too wanted to fly away, though not knowing why . . .
>
> ["I walked all day yesterday"]

Here is another example, in which he compares capital growth based upon the exploitation of labor to a golden spider.

> Mother, I'm scared
> the golden spider will eat us,
> and spin out white thread
>
> ["in front of the golden spider"]

These lines show that his sensations are fundamentally existential agonies.

Yi's poetic self responds with equal attention to everything he perceives or imagines—fields, wild grass, the river of death, etc. The voice of the poetic self is particularly beautiful when singing of poverty, of mother, of abandoning the world.

> the grass that grows at the bottom of the river, the grass that
> runs, the grass that glides
> becomes grotesque dreams
> the day nameless flowers climbing the ridgelines of the
> hills dipped their heads, tired, and fell asleep,
>
> and the little kids playing in the street, mother's milk still on
>   their lips,
> tired of their humdrum games paused, and gazed off into the
>   distance
>
> look, there, she's coming
> and my mother, returning with almost nothing
> having sold pieces of our worn furniture pieces to the junk
>   dealer,
> lay down on our narrow wooden strip of porch and rested her
>   head on her basket,
>
> flowers bloomed like a rash throughout the village
> and the reek of poverty pierced our noses
>   ["the grass that grows at the bottom of the river"]

The poverty depicted here is not the hopeless kind—poverty as an accursed pattern of life— that would rouse people to rise up and fight against it, but simply poverty as it is. The poem gives expression to the pain of living in such a condition. One can take issue with Yi's depictions of poverty as revealing a lack of will to fight against it—as in the little kids who, "tired of their humdrum games paused, and gazed off into the distance." Or one can claim, as did An Pyŏngmu, that "the poor should be treated as self-reliant people who can save themselves, and not as people who are in need of being saved." But these objections do not undermine the values of the poem. First, though the poor are not the saviors themselves, they do provide the medium from which salvation will come, so that those who are poor of heart can also be saved! Second, poems that can make the upper middle class more aware of the condition of those who live in poverty, and more ashamed of themselves, are as important as poems that remind farmers and laborers of their own poverty.

But I'm much more drawn to Yi's poems about the mother—those songs about being abandoned by the world—than I am to his poems about poverty. To me, his poetic imagination seems more at home in the poems about the mother.

> my beloved mother is getting wet
> my beloved mother is sinking in water
> she doesn't make the slightest movement
> even when the water penetrates her skin and her body swells
> she doesn't make the slightest movement
> even when the rainwater seeps deep inside her eyes
> and creeps into her ears, forming legions of droplets
> even when the weeds beneath her feet grow over her head and
>   the acacia roots
> fan out inside her mouth   my mother,
> her hot breath blows toward me
>
> even when I close the window, and plug my ears,
> I still hear the sound of rain
> my beloved mother is getting wet in the rain
> my beloved mother is sinking in water
>
> > ["when it rains again"]

This mother is a mother whom one can meet in life. She is also an earth mother, who exists as a principle or condition of life.

This mother "doesn't make the slightest movement" no matter what kind of disaster afflicts her. Yi is describing the acceptances, agonies, and depressions of the mother by transferring them to the earthy material image of rain. Without the slightest movement, the mother accepts "the sound of rain," which can be heard even after the narrator closes the window. She is the very principle of the acceptance of a life of pain. Is such acceptance simply resignation? I am aware that many people think so. I am also aware that, subconsciously and in their own way they also are resigned to accepting life as they find it. People cannot possibly stay tuned-in twenty-four hours a day. To resist, at some point they have to rest. The mother provides a steadfast refuge within which one can rest and relax in the ongoing struggle to remain keenly attentive.

But even given such a mother, the world is a place that Yi sometimes wants to abandon.

> crossing the Jordan, that autumnal color
> a wooden rowboat flattens the waves
> my heart is like that boat . . .
>
> that flame will be extinguished, it will be extinguished
> and after it is extinguished
> I'll console someone   and by lying be consoled
>   ["crossing the Jordan, that autumnal color"]

His heart is like a boat crossing the Jordan, and like the autumnal flame that is about to be extinguished. Although he draws upon Western images—the river Jordan and the autumnal flame—the image of the flame of life that will soon be extinguished does touch our hearts with sadness. The sadness is exactly what we see in "a life of deepening loneliness" [*from* "watermelon"]. Underlying this sadness is an outcry of longing to die, which sometimes does happen. I guess our hearts are truly "uncontrollably lonely" [*from* "his heart is uncontrollably lonely"].

Notes to *When Does a Rolling Stone Awaken*

Page
Numbered

15   **South Pacific.** Japan forcibly annexed Korea in 1910 and ruled it until the end of World War Two. Koreans were made to serve in the Japanese armed forces.

      salacious picture. Yi used the word *ch'unhwa* (춘화, 春畫), which though having a literal meaning of "spring pictures," is also a euphemism for graphic material of a sexual or pornographic nature, such as Japanese "shunga" painting.

17   **"in a congenial brothel."** Yi's poetry began appearing in Korean literary magazines in the late 1970s. This was his first poem to be published, in 1977. "In a congenial brothel" was supposedly his title of choice for this book.

      Eli, Eli. An allusion to Matthew 27:46.

23   **Hugŭm** (후금, 後金). This is likely a reference to one of the "barbarian" *Houjin* Manchurian tribal groups that may have settled in Koguryŏ, the northernmost of the three kingdoms of ancient Korea. The *Houjin*, like the Malgals and Huns mentioned in the next poem, are possibly ancestors of modern Koreans.

      ttŏk (떡). Sweets made from cooked glutinous rice that is pounded to a paste and then formed into various bite-sized shapes, some coated with soy or acorn powder, others filled with sweet bean paste. The Japanese equivalent is *mochi*.

25 ***Malgals* and *Huns*.** Nomadic tribes, probably of Asian ethnicity, that at least from as early as the fourth century CE were living along the northern and western borders of China. The Malgals are thought to be the ancestors of the Jurchens of Manchuria, and of the Manchus, who in the seventeenth century conquered China. It is also possible that the Malgals settled in Korea, in Koguryŏ, the northern part of the country. The Huns are probably not of the ethnic group that under Attila invaded Europe.

37 **Mongol troops.** Yi uses the word *Oemonggo* (외몽고, 外蒙古), which translates literally as "Outer-Mongolian."

39 **Neva River**. St. Petersburg's river. In the poem it is probably meant to suggest the Han River, which flows through Seoul, and to allude to Dostoevsky and/or Mandelstam. Both lived and wrote in St. Petersburg, both were subjected to persecution by a repressive government, and both were favorites of and influenced Yi.

47 ***mu*** (무). The long white tubular Asian variety of radish. *Daikon* in Japanese.

49 **Ahyŏn-dong** (아현동). A neighborhood in the northwestern part of Seoul.

veranda. maru (마루). A wooden platform outside the rooms of a traditional Korean house. People remove their shoes there before entering the house, and will also sit and talk there.

59 **Kŭmch'on** (금촌). There are several localities of that name in South Korea. Yi is almost certainly referring to the Kŭmch'on north of Seoul, and not too far from the part of the city where he and his family lived after moving from the town of Sangju in the south of the country (see the following poem, "flowering dad").

65 **P'aju** (파주). A small township north of Seoul near the Demilitarized Zone.

I Heard Life Calling Me

li (리). A Chinese measurement of distance, equal to roughly five hundred yards.

75   **Haran.** A small village in southeastern Turkey that has been inhabited for at least four thousand years. In Babylonian times it was a center of worship of the moon god Sin. It is mentioned in the "Genesis" section of the Old Testament: Abraham spent time there on his way from Ur to Canaan; Isaac's wife Rebecca was from Haran; Jacob, after running away from his brother Esau's death threat, lived there for twenty years, and all his children, except Benjamin, were born there.

77   **Moraenae, Hwagok-dong** (모래내,화곡동). Neighborhoods in the western part of Seoul where Yi's family lived after leaving the Sangju area.

81   **Pyŏkjae** (벽제). A town north of Seoul, site of a crematorium.

85   **Sinch'on** (신촌). A densely populated shopping and student area just west of the center of Seoul. The campuses of Yonsei University, Ewha Woman's University, and Sogang University are located in Sinch'on.

91   **Cheju** (제주) **Island.** A large island some 180 miles south of the mainland. The Cheju native pony stands some eleven hands high and is used for light draft work and riding.

sautéed silkworm larvae (*pŏndaegi,* 번데기). A popular snack sold by street vendors.

Ch'anggyŏng (창경) **Palace.** One of the oldest royal palaces in Seoul. Built in 1418, rebuilt after being destroyed during the Japanese invasion of 1592. According to news reports, people have been found abandoned by their families on palace grounds and in other such places.

93   **Gregor Samsa.** The protagonist of Franz Kafka's short story "Metamorphosis."

95   *toenjang* (된장). A Korean soybean paste similar to Japanese *miso* that is used as a base for soups and as a seasoning in the preparation and con-

sumption of many foods. Before being produced and sold commercially, it was made at home and stored outside in large earthenware crocks.

devour your mother. A colloquial expression used by parents to chastise children for bad behavior.

99   **teachers become fish.** A play on the words for teacher (*sŏnsaeng*, 선생) and fish (*saengsŏn*, 생선).

101   **Sakhalin.** A large island north of Hokkaido and off the east coast of Siberia. From 1904 until the end of World War Two the northern part of the island was Russian/Soviet territory, the southern part Japanese. In 1944 the Japanese transported some 45,000 Koreans there as slave laborers. When the war ended the Soviet Union took control of the Japanese part of the island. In the ensuing Cold War, the Koreans still alive were left in a political limbo, unseen, unheard from, forgotten.

103   *soju* (소주). An inexpensive, widely and heavily consumed traditional Korean alcoholic spirit (20%–40% by volume), normally distilled from rice and/or potatoes, sweet potatoes, wheat, barley.

105   **Pavese** (Cesare). Italian novelist, poet, translator, literary critic. He strongly influenced Yi Sŏng-bok, as did Paul Celan, who also committed suicide.

125   *ttŏk* (떡). See note for page 23.

127   *yŏnt'an* (연탄). Cylindrical coal briquettes, weighing approximately eight pounds, which until recently served as the primary fuel for heating homes and for cooking.

129   **the bus for home.** The curfew in Seoul required people to be off the streets by midnight. Buses would begin their final trip around eleven.

129   **Hundredth-day photo.** Traditionally, Koreans celebrate the hundredth day after birth of infants. The custom probably originated when infant

mortality was high. Infants surviving the first hundred days were considered to have a good chance to continue to survive.

131 *Two-p'yŏng* **room**. In the United States, the area of a room or a house is given in square feet. In Korea, the unit of measurement is *p'yŏng* (평), approximately 3.3 square meters—roughly ten square feet.

139 **unmarketable *mu*** (무). When harvesting radishes, farmers leave behind in the field those damaged on being dug up.

143 **whenever coins fall**. From hands that give to the poor and the crippled begging on the streets.

yŏnt'an (연탄) **stove**. See note for page 127. Most stoves were not vented. Every winter there were individuals and families who died from carbon monoxide poisoning.

soju (소주). See note for page 103.

Notes to *South Sea, Silk Mountain*

Page
Numbered

161 **Tess.** The inspiration for the poem was possibly Roman Polanski's 1979 film *Tess*, adapted from Thomas Hardy's novel *Tess of the d'Urbervilles*.

163 **noodles of memory.** Korean buckwheat noodles, *makguksu* (막국수), eaten cold with various toppings.

165 ***ttŏk*** (떡). Sweets made from cooked glutinous rice pounded to a paste and then formed into various bite-sized shapes, some coated with soy or acorn powder, others filled with sweet bean paste. The Japanese equivalent is *mochi*.

167 **pressed pig's head.** A Korean delicacy, *nŭllin toeji mŏri* (눌린 돼지 머리), made by boiling the head of a pig, stripping the meat from the skull, and then compacting the meat beneath a heavy weight.

175 **the sick lying in their beds.** Koreans have traditionally slept on the floor upon cotton mats.

183 ***ttŏk***. See above.

187 ***chapch'ae*** (잡채). A Korean stir-fried noodle, beef, and vegetable dish. The noodles, made from mung bean starch, are variously referred to as pea-starch, bean-thread, glass, or cellophane noodles. They are fine-textured. After being cooked they are transparent, and extremely slippery.

193 **breasts shaped like burial mounds.** Traditional burial is in hillside graves, called *mudŏm* (무덤). A cone-shaped (breast-shaped) mound of earth is built up over the grave. Korean hillsides are covered with burial mounds.

199 ***paduk*** (바둑). A four-thousand year old Asian board game (*weiqi* in Chinese, *go* in Japanese) played with small beveled black and white "stones."

CORNELL EAST ASIA SERIES

CORNELL
East Asia Series

Order online at www.einaudi.cornell.edu/eastasia/publications or contact
Cornell University Press Services, P. O. Box 6525, 750 Cascadilla Street,
Ithaca, NY 14851, USA.
Tel: 1-800-666-2211 (USA or Canada), 1-607-277-2211 (International);
Fax: 1-800-688-2877 (USA or Canada), 1-607-277-6292 (International);
E-mail orders: orderbook@cupserv.org

CPSIA information can be obtained
at www.ICGtesting.com
Printed in the USA
LVHW111926131119
637261LV00006B/14/P